SUNDAY

IN THE

PARK

WITH

BOYS

PUBLISHED BY KOYAMA PRESS

SECOND EDITION!

WWW.JANEMAI.CO
WWW.KOYAMAPRESS.COM

PRINTED IN CHINA

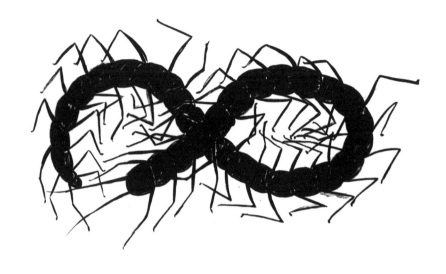

ISBN: 978-0-9879630-5-5

FOR MY FRIENDS WHO PUT UP WITH MY SHIT,
FOR STINKY WHO SOLVES ALL MY PROBLEMS
AND FOR MY PARENTS WHO LOVE ME
EVEN IF THEY DON'T UNDERSTAND ME

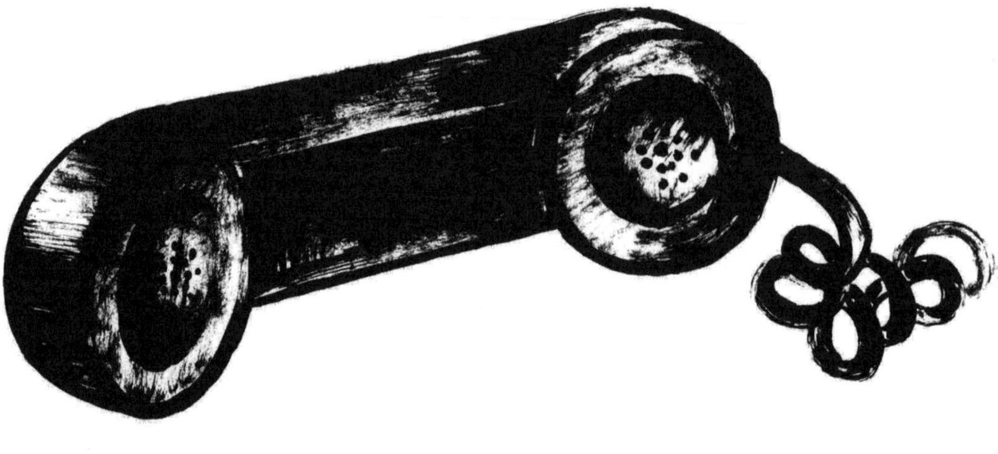

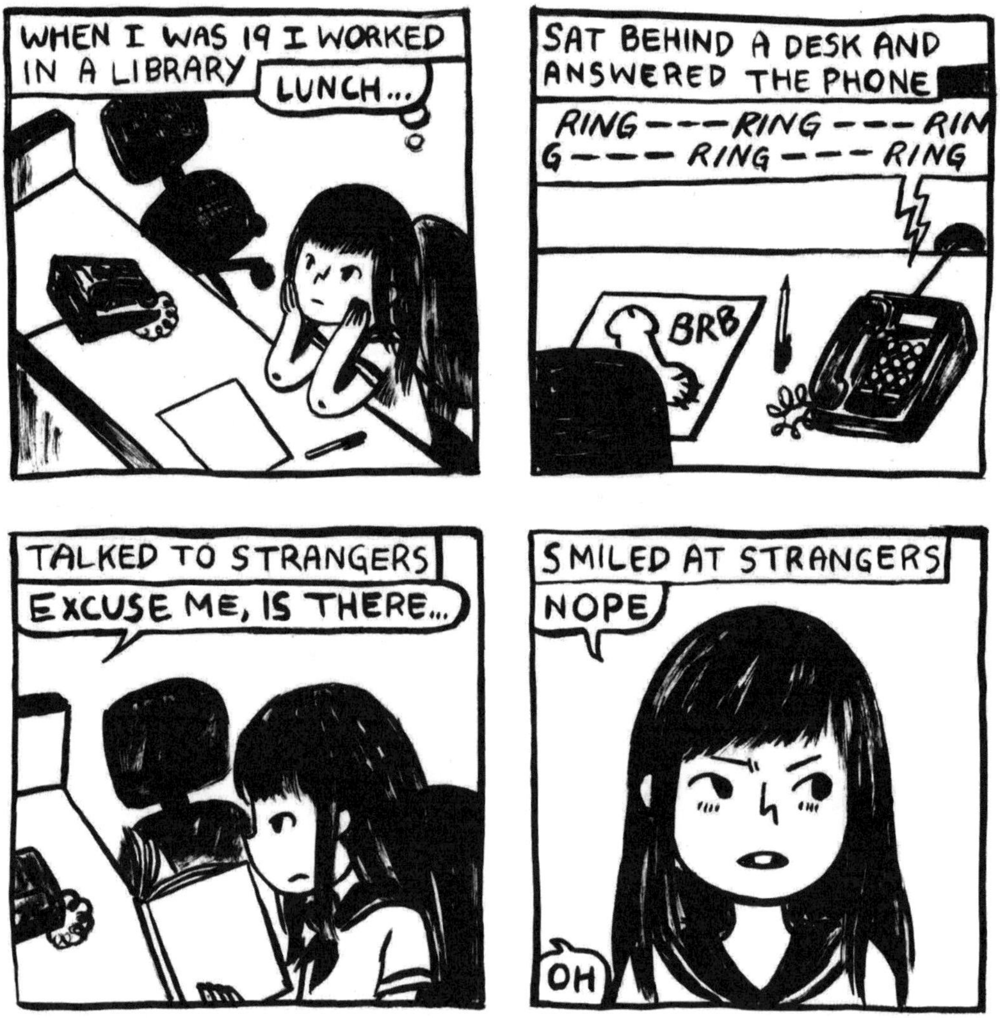
WHEN I WAS 19 I WORKED IN A LIBRARY
LUNCH...
SAT BEHIND A DESK AND ANSWERED THE PHONE
RING---RING---RIN
G---RING---RING
BRB
TALKED TO STRANGERS
EXCUSE ME, IS THERE...
SMILED AT STRANGERS
NOPE
OH

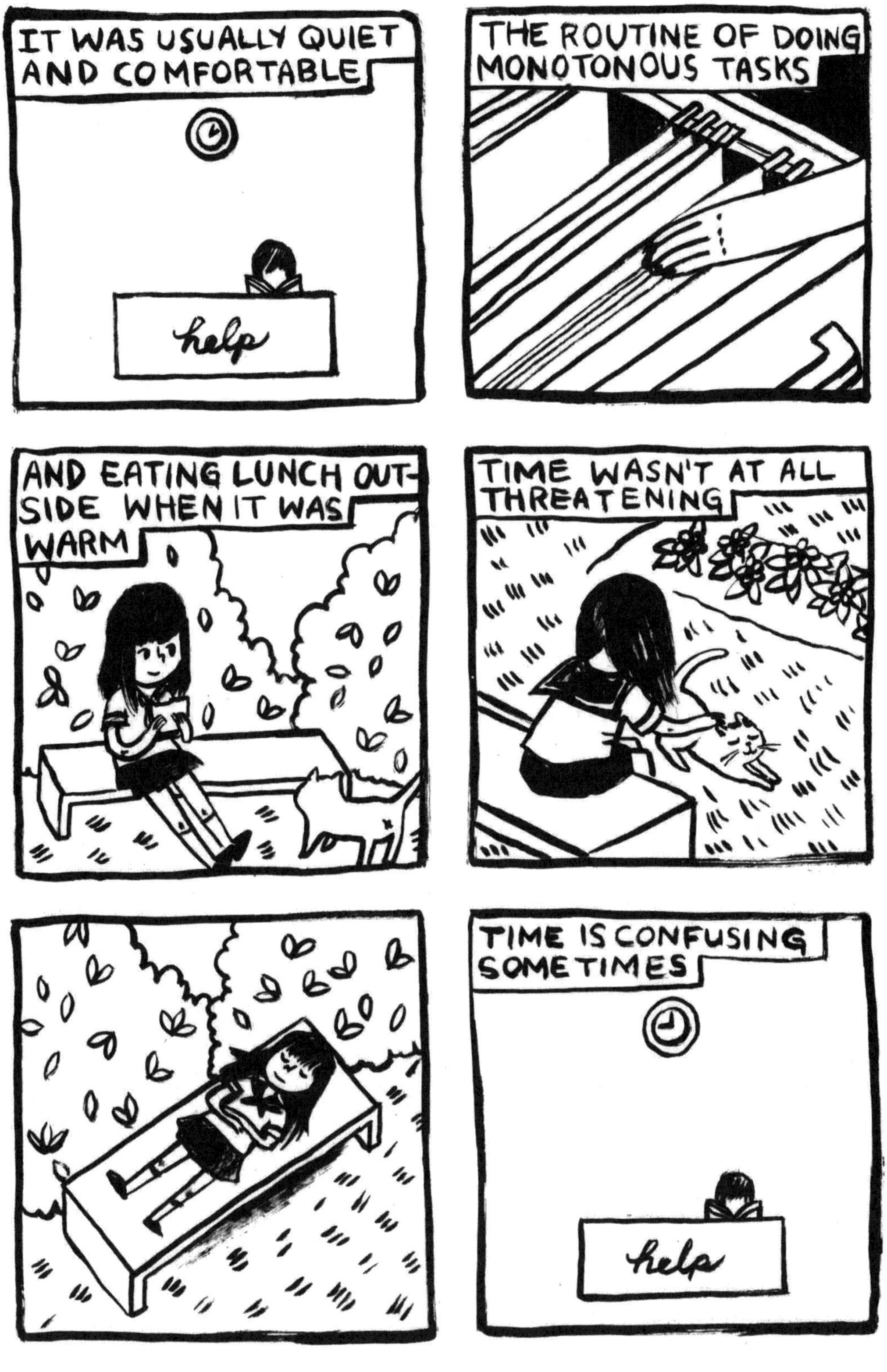
IT WAS USUALLY QUIET AND COMFORTABLE
help
THE ROUTINE OF DOING MONOTONOUS TASKS
AND EATING LUNCH OUT-SIDE WHEN IT WAS WARM
TIME WASN'T AT ALL THREATENING
TIME IS CONFUSING SOMETIMES
help

I READ A LOT AT WORK SINCE THE STACKS WERE RIGHT THERE

THE STACKS WERE BEAUTIFUL

THE FLOORS WERE MADE OF GLASS

I HAD MY FIRST EXISTENTIAL CRISIS IN THERE

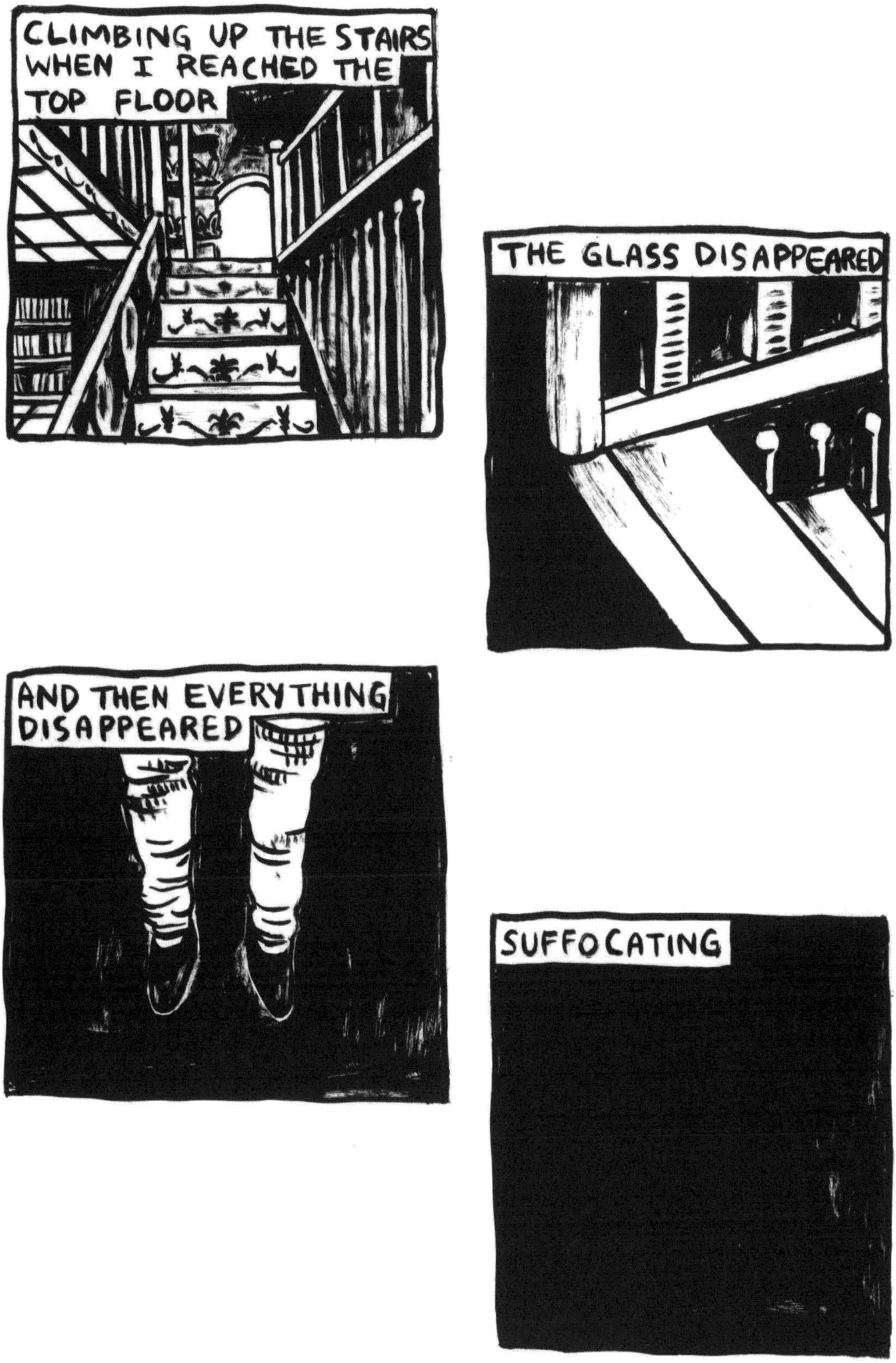
CLIMBING UP THE STAIRS WHEN I REACHED THE TOP FLOOR
THE GLASS DISAPPEARED
AND THEN EVERYTHING DISAPPEARED
SUFFOCATING

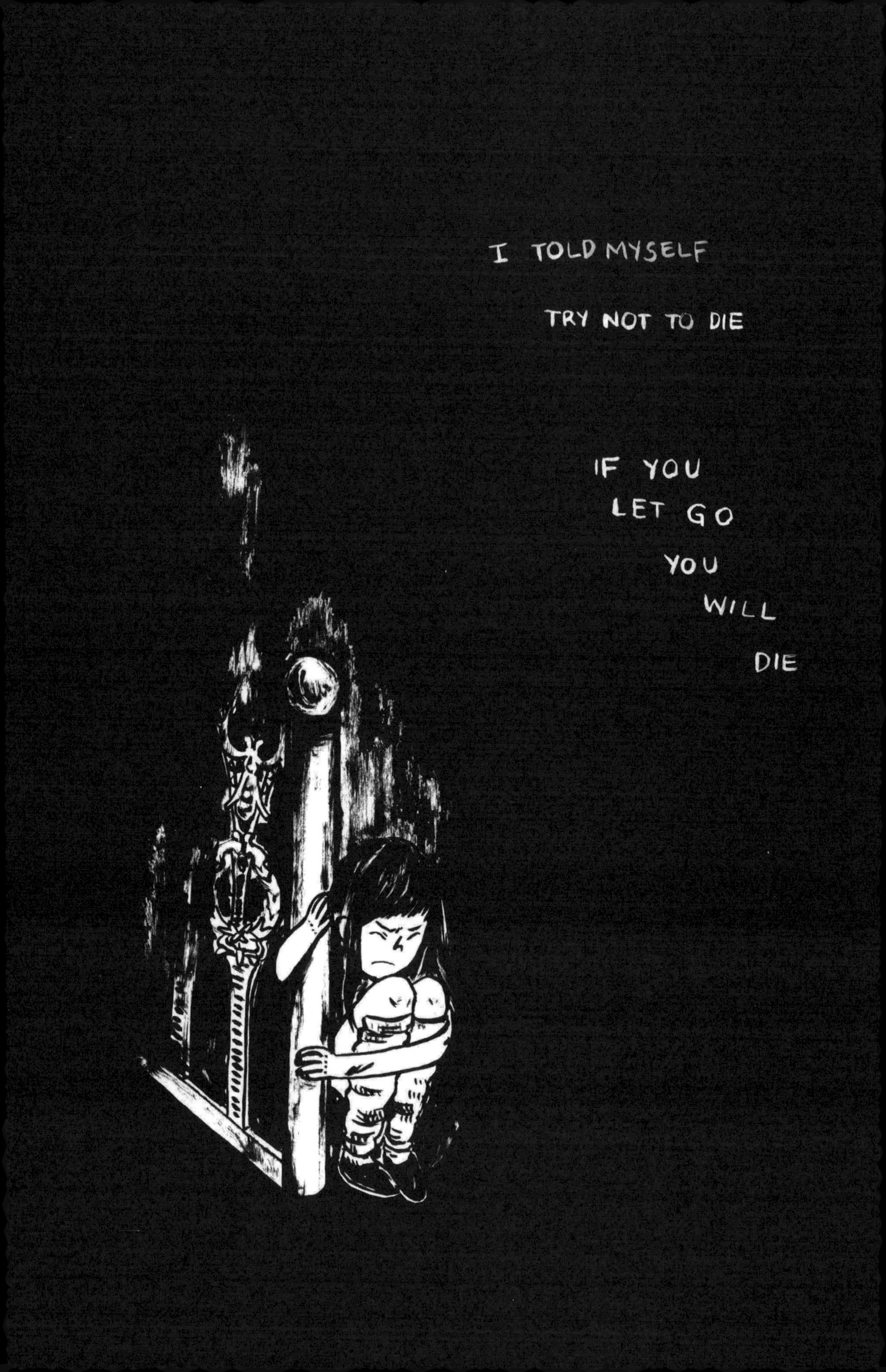
I TOLD MYSELF
TRY NOT TO DIE
IF YOU
LET GO
YOU
WILL
DIE

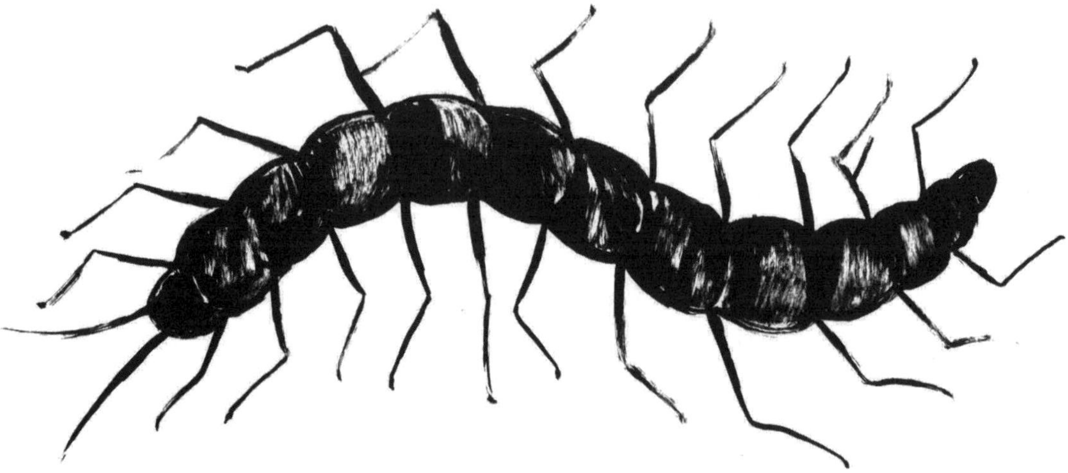

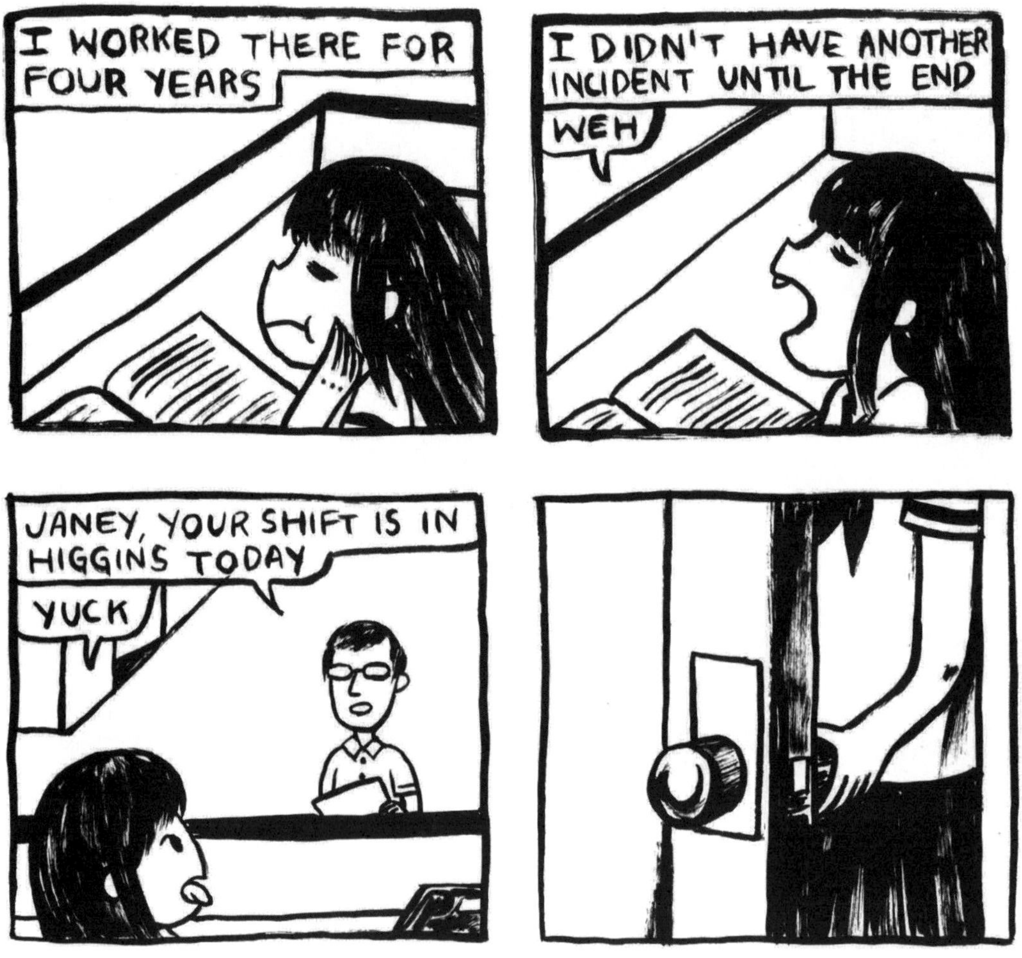
I WORKED THERE FOR FOUR YEARS
I DIDN'T HAVE ANOTHER INCIDENT UNTIL THE END
WEH
JANEY, YOUR SHIFT IS IN HIGGINS TODAY
YUCK

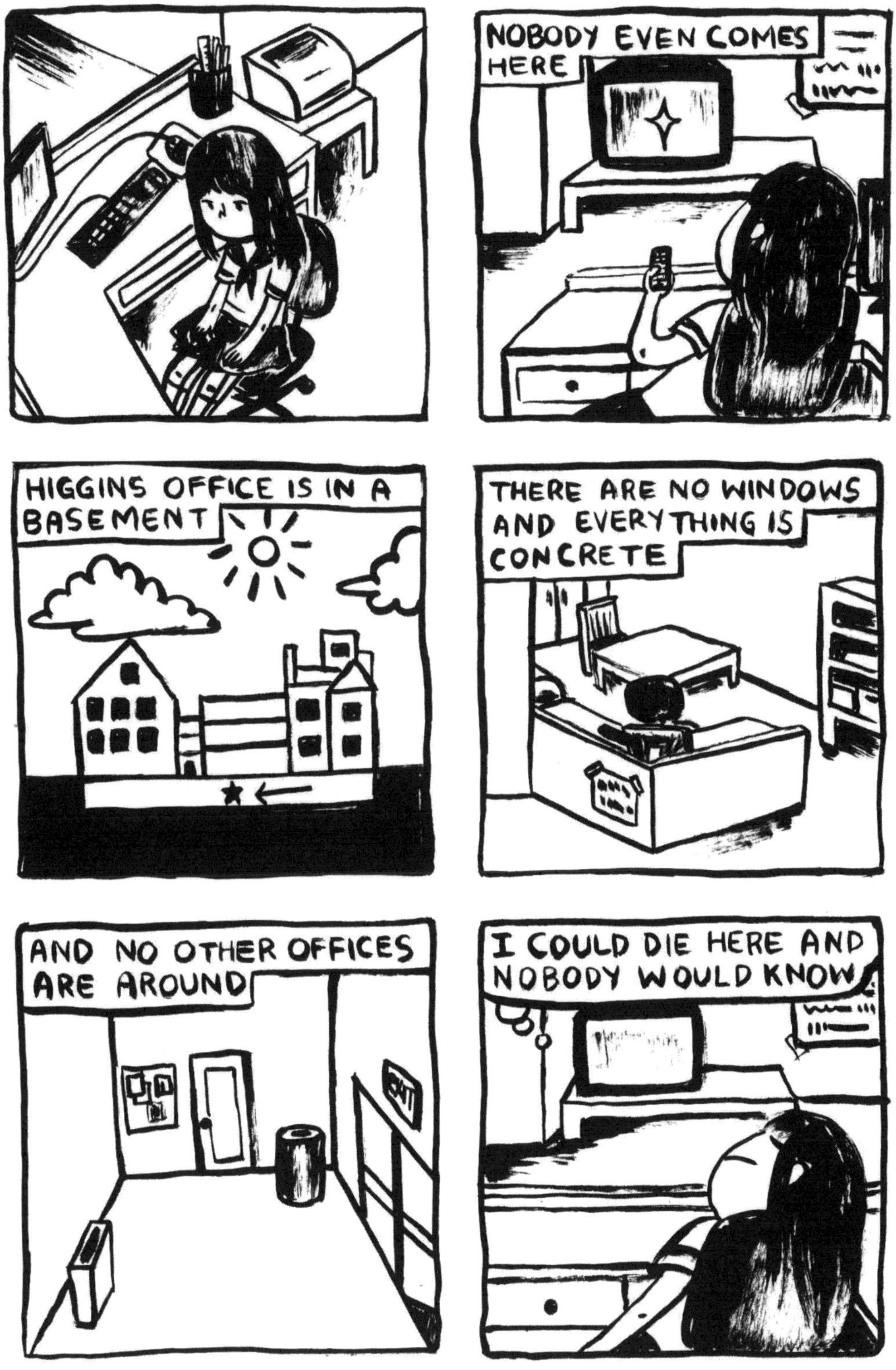
NOBODY EVEN COMES HERE
HIGGINS OFFICE IS IN A BASEMENT
THERE ARE NO WINDOWS AND EVERYTHING IS CONCRETE
AND NO OTHER OFFICES ARE AROUND
I COULD DIE HERE AND NOBODY WOULD KNOW

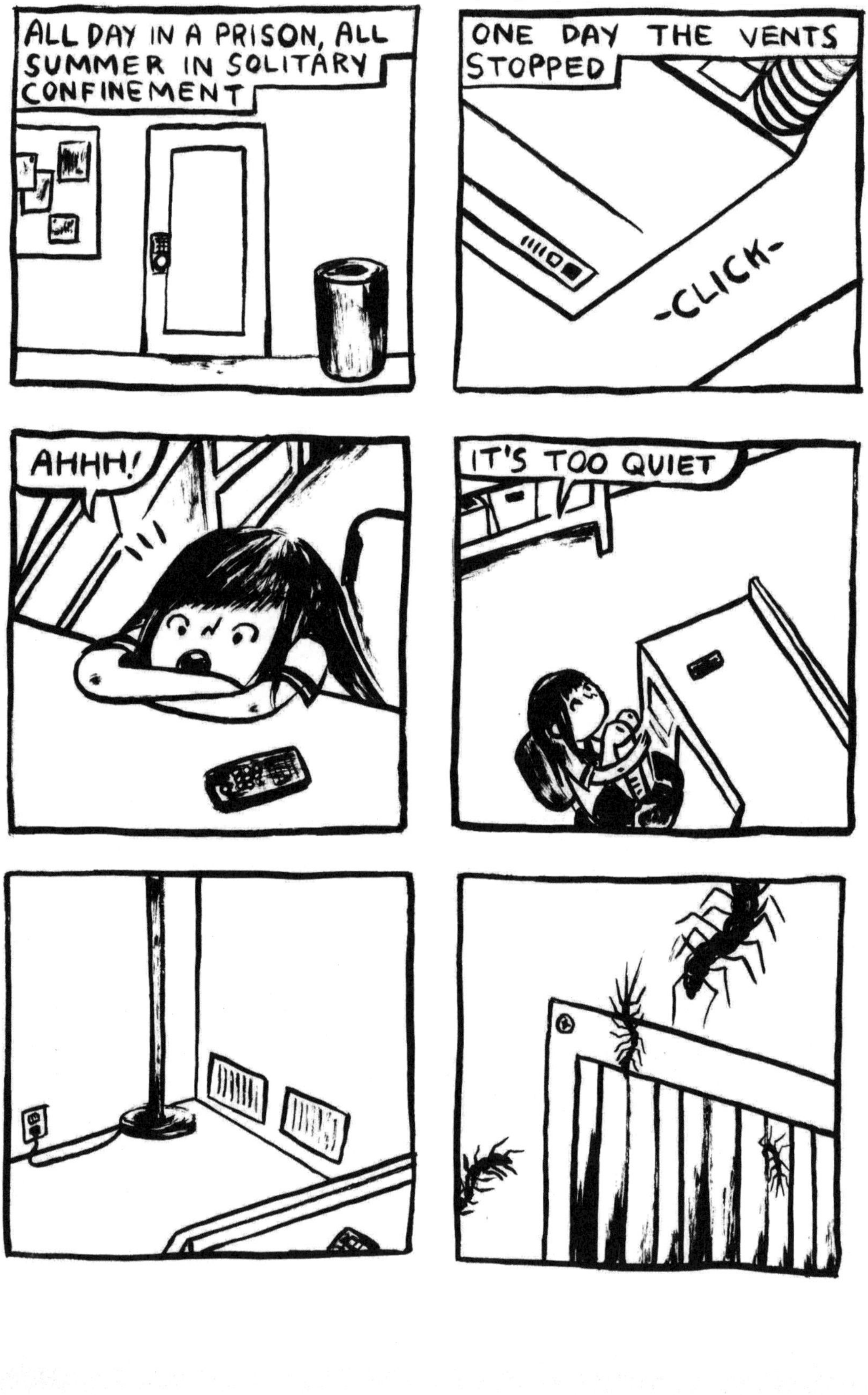
ALL DAY IN A PRISON, ALL SUMMER IN SOLITARY CONFINEMENT
ONE DAY THE VENTS STOPPED
-CLICK-
AHHH!
IT'S TOO QUIET

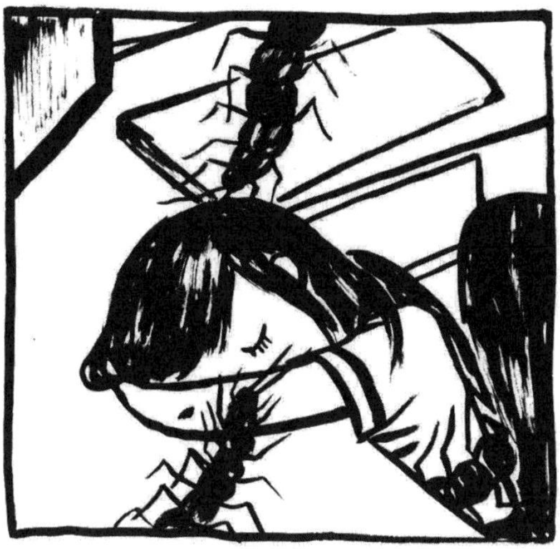

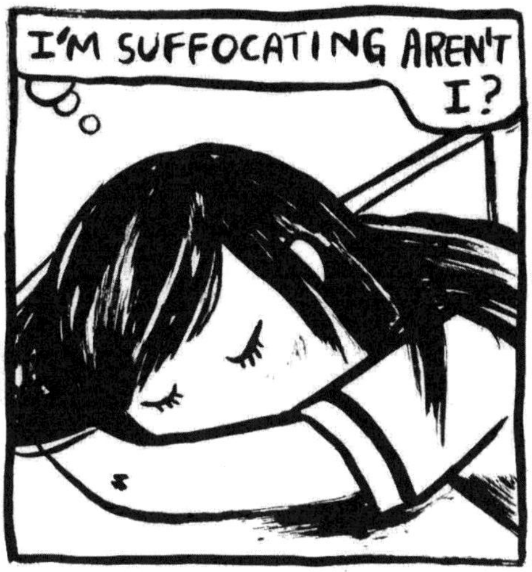
I'M SUFFOCATING AREN'T I?

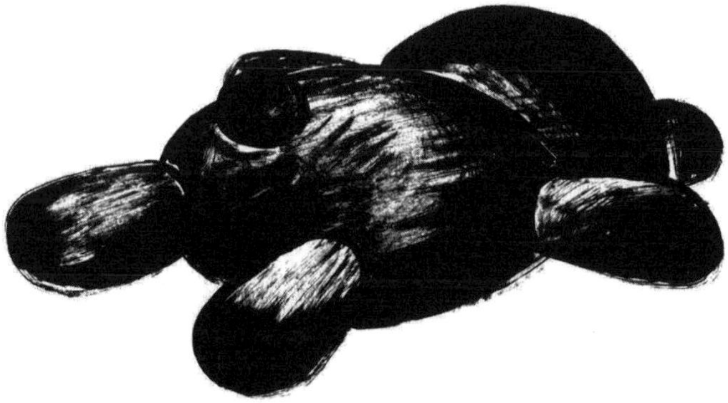

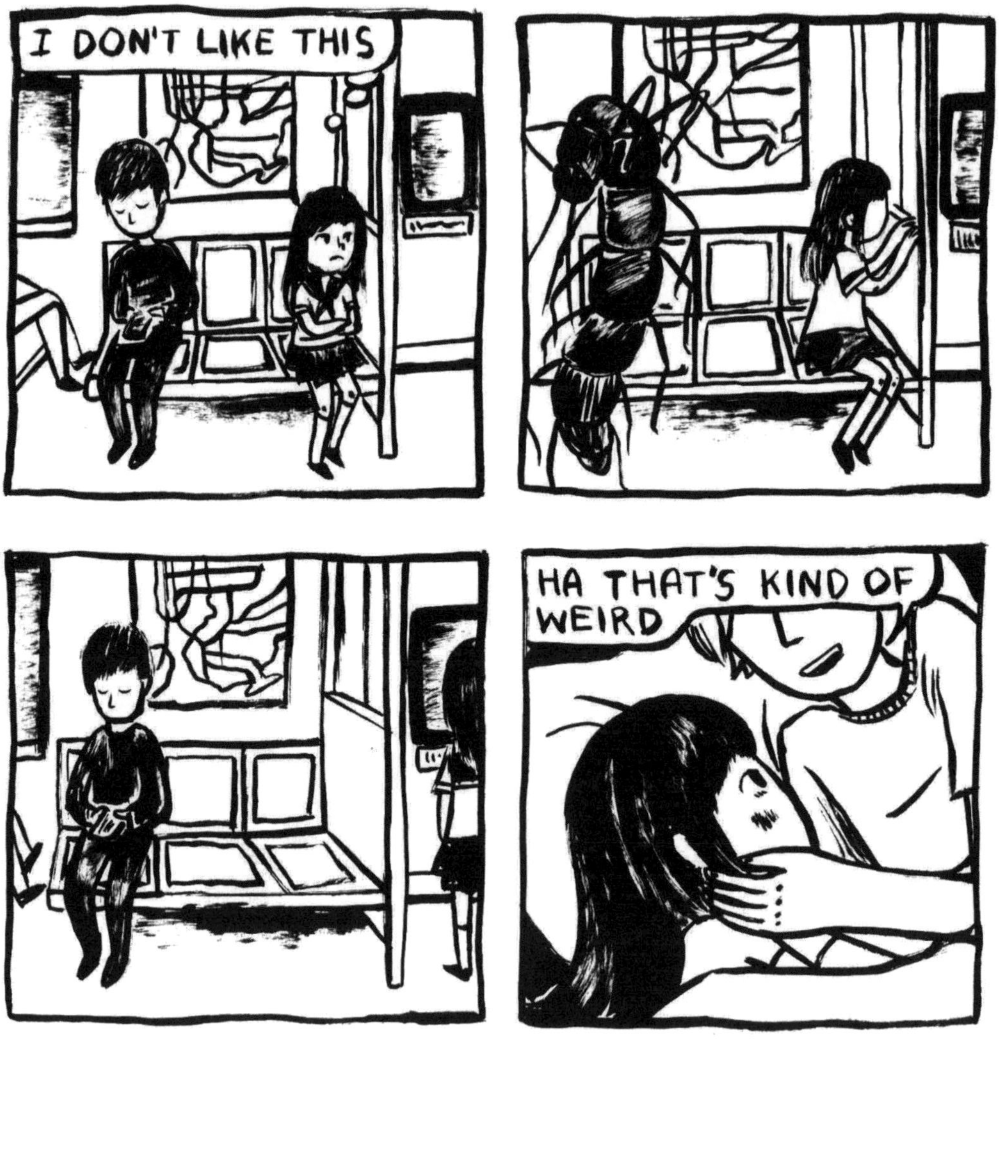
I DON'T LIKE THIS
HA THAT'S KIND OF WEIRD

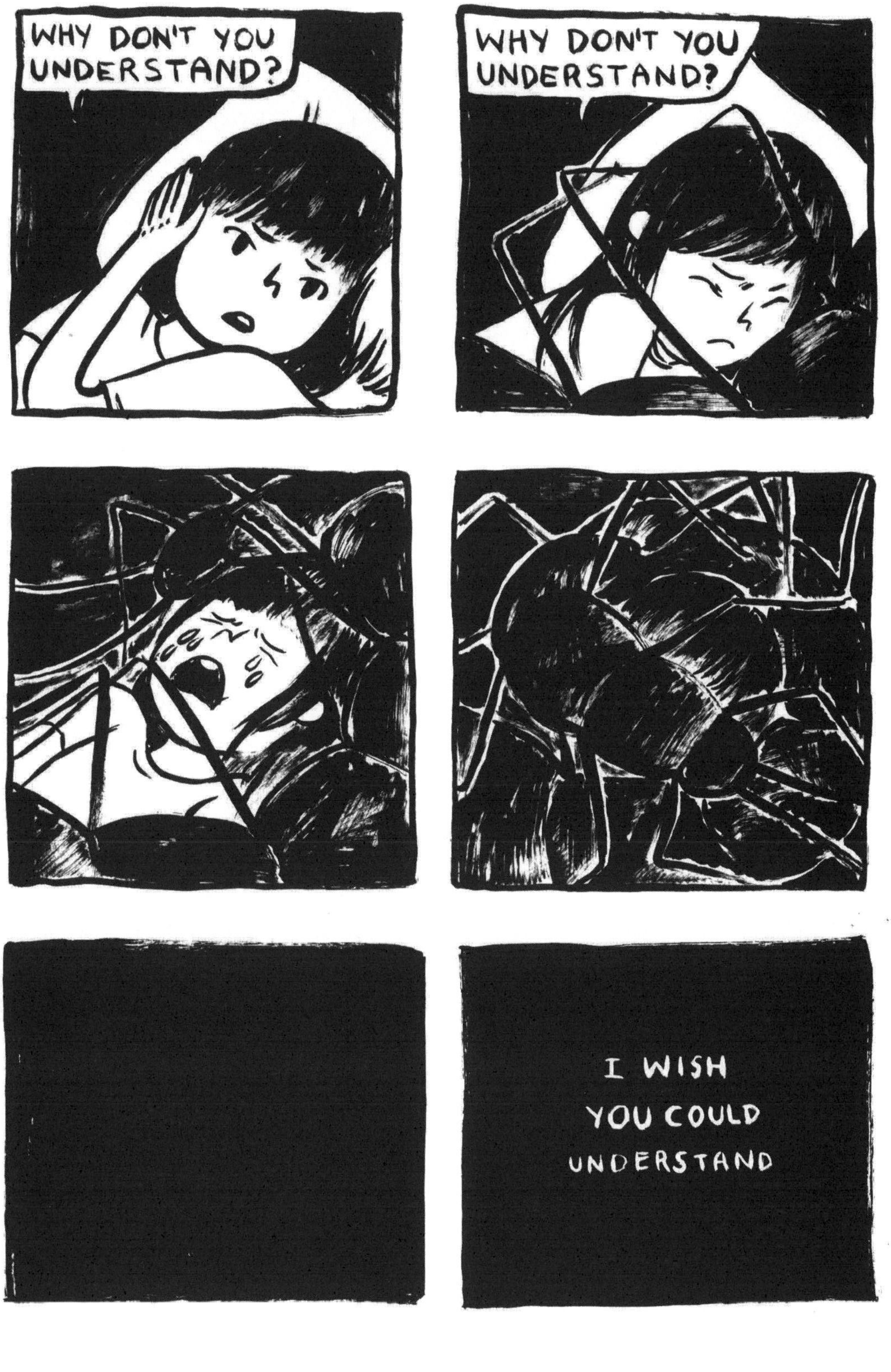
WHY DON'T YOU UNDERSTAND?
WHY DON'T YOU UNDERSTAND?
I WISH YOU COULD UNDERSTAND

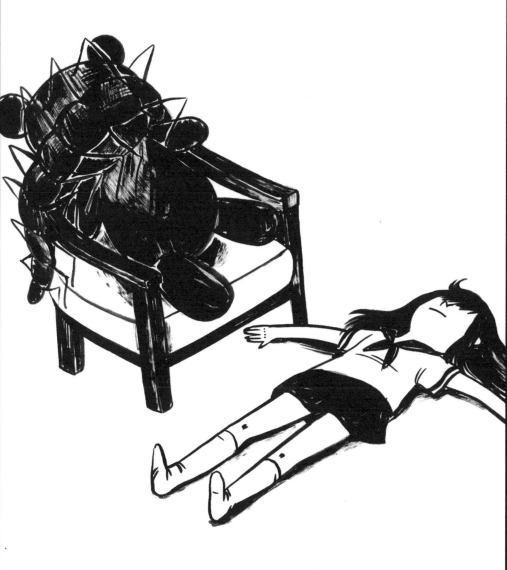

I'M VERY, VERY TIRED

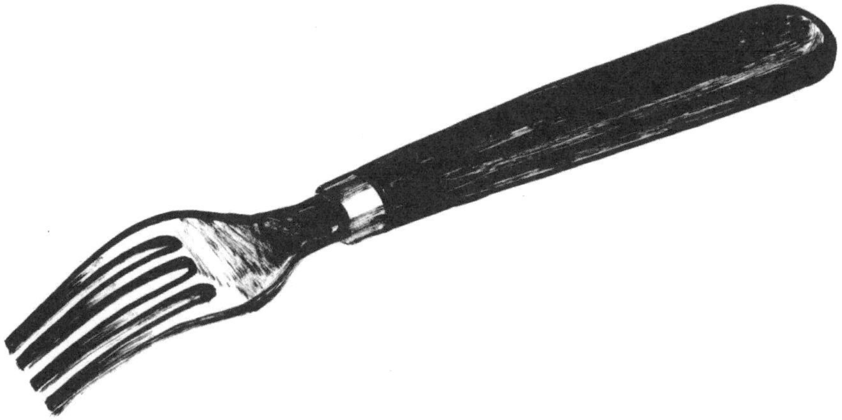

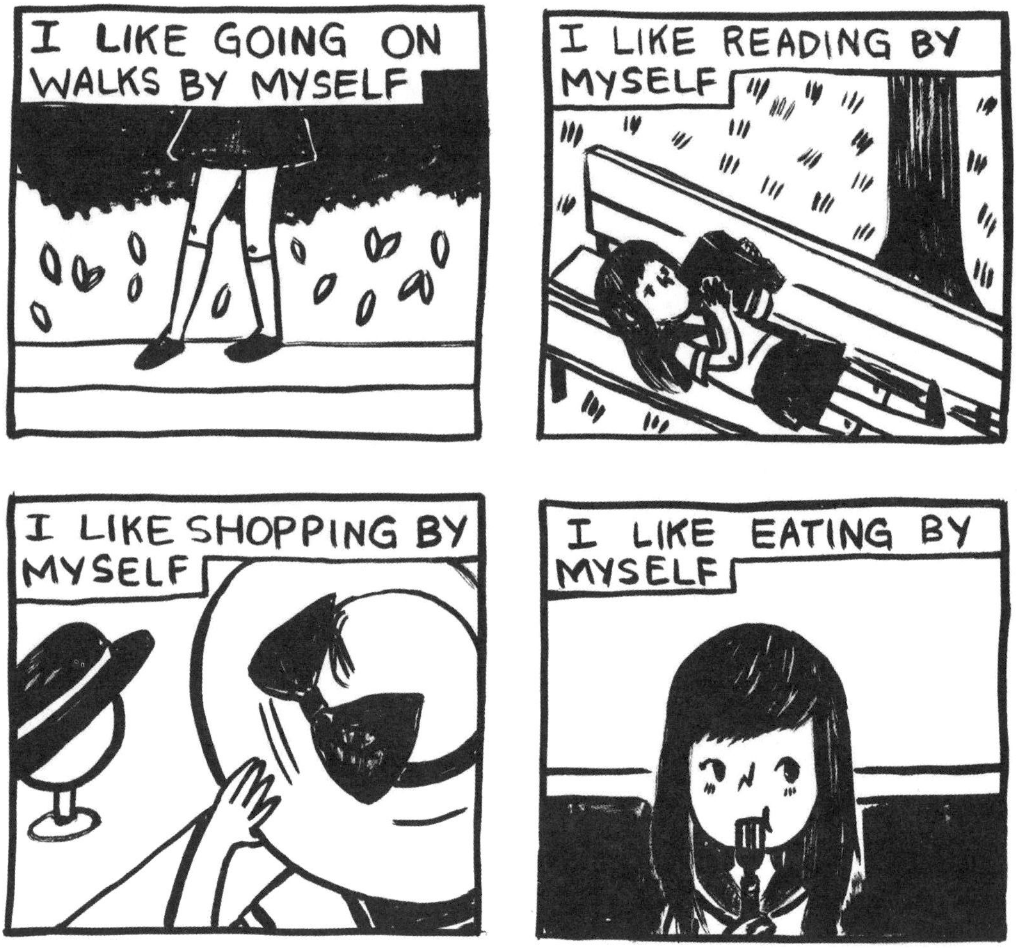
I LIKE GOING ON WALKS BY MYSELF
I LIKE READING BY MYSELF
I LIKE SHOPPING BY MYSELF
I LIKE EATING BY MYSELF

I LIKE BEING BY MYSELF
I LIKE BEING ALONE
I LIKE BEING ALONE
I LIKE BEING ALONE

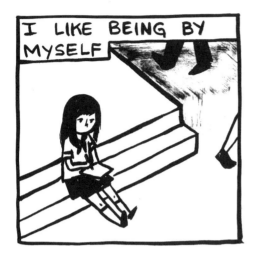

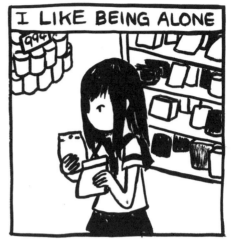

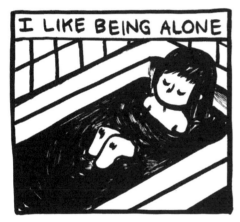

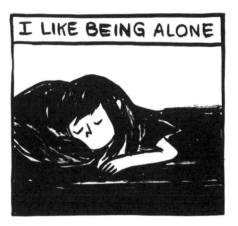

I HATE BEING ALONE

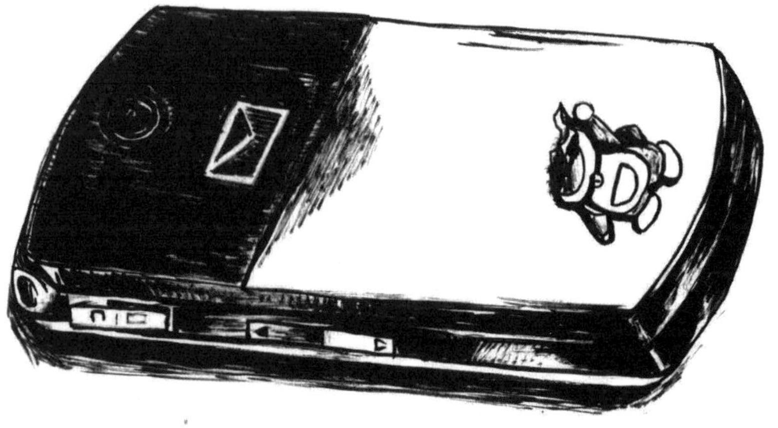

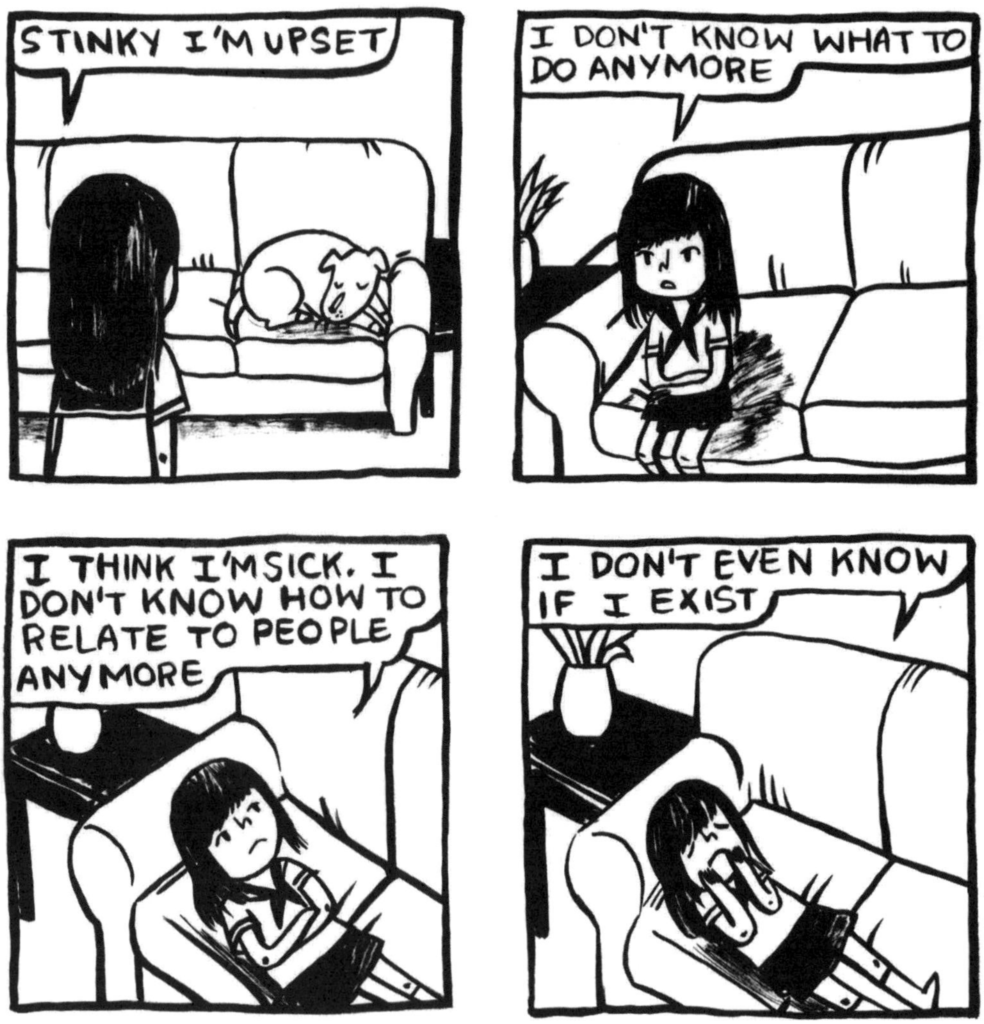
STINKY I'M UPSET
I DON'T KNOW WHAT TO DO ANYMORE
I THINK I'M SICK. I DON'T KNOW HOW TO RELATE TO PEOPLE ANYMORE
I DON'T EVEN KNOW IF I EXIST

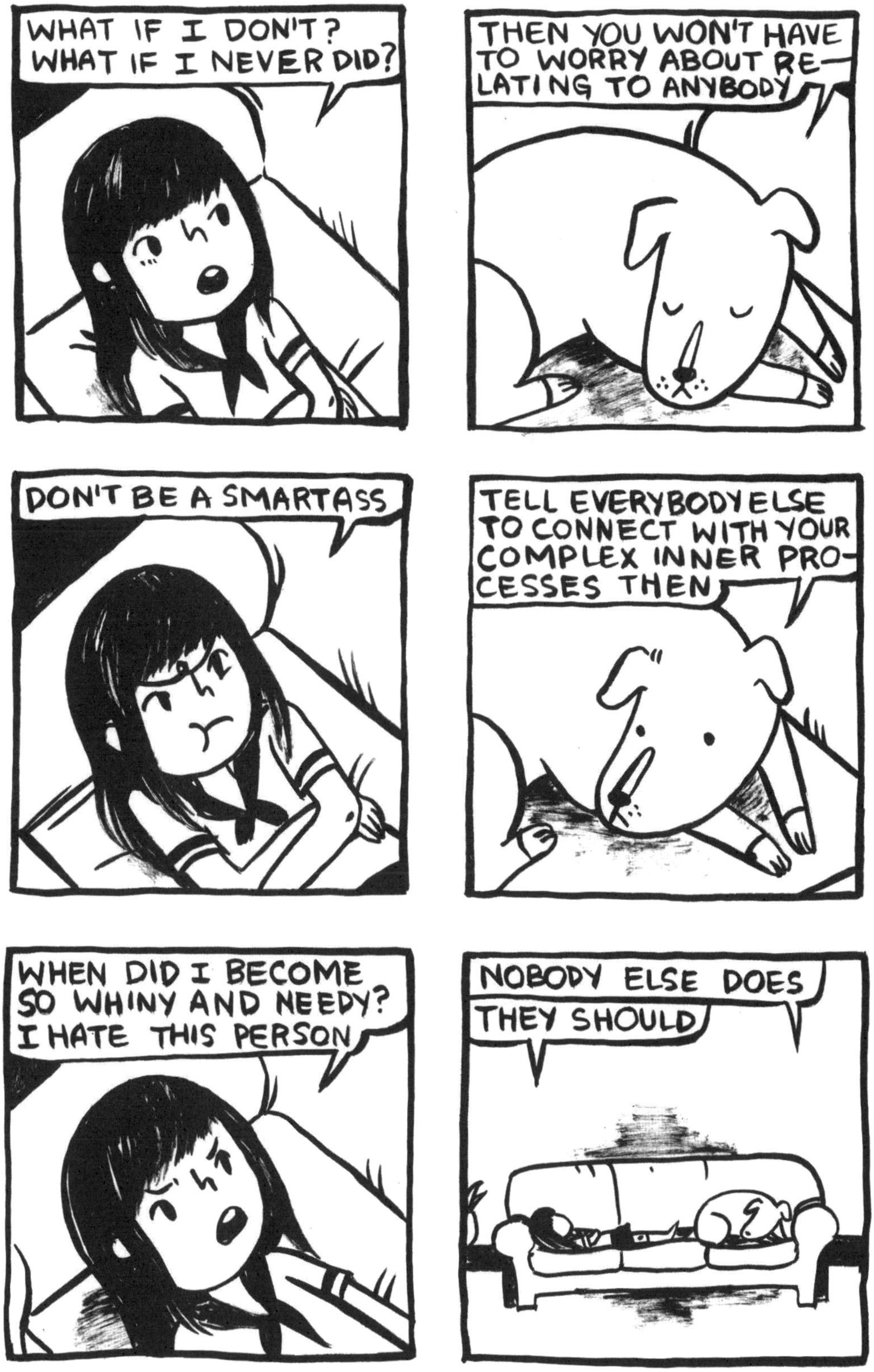
WHAT IF I DON'T? WHAT IF I NEVER DID?
THEN YOU WON'T HAVE TO WORRY ABOUT RE-LATING TO ANYBODY
DON'T BE A SMARTASS
TELL EVERYBODY ELSE TO CONNECT WITH YOUR COMPLEX INNER PRO-CESSES THEN
WHEN DID I BECOME SO WHINY AND NEEDY? I HATE THIS PERSON
NOBODY ELSE DOES
THEY SHOULD

CANIS MINOR

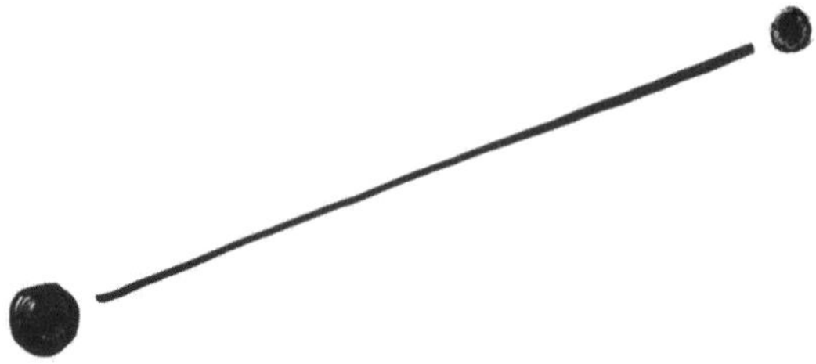

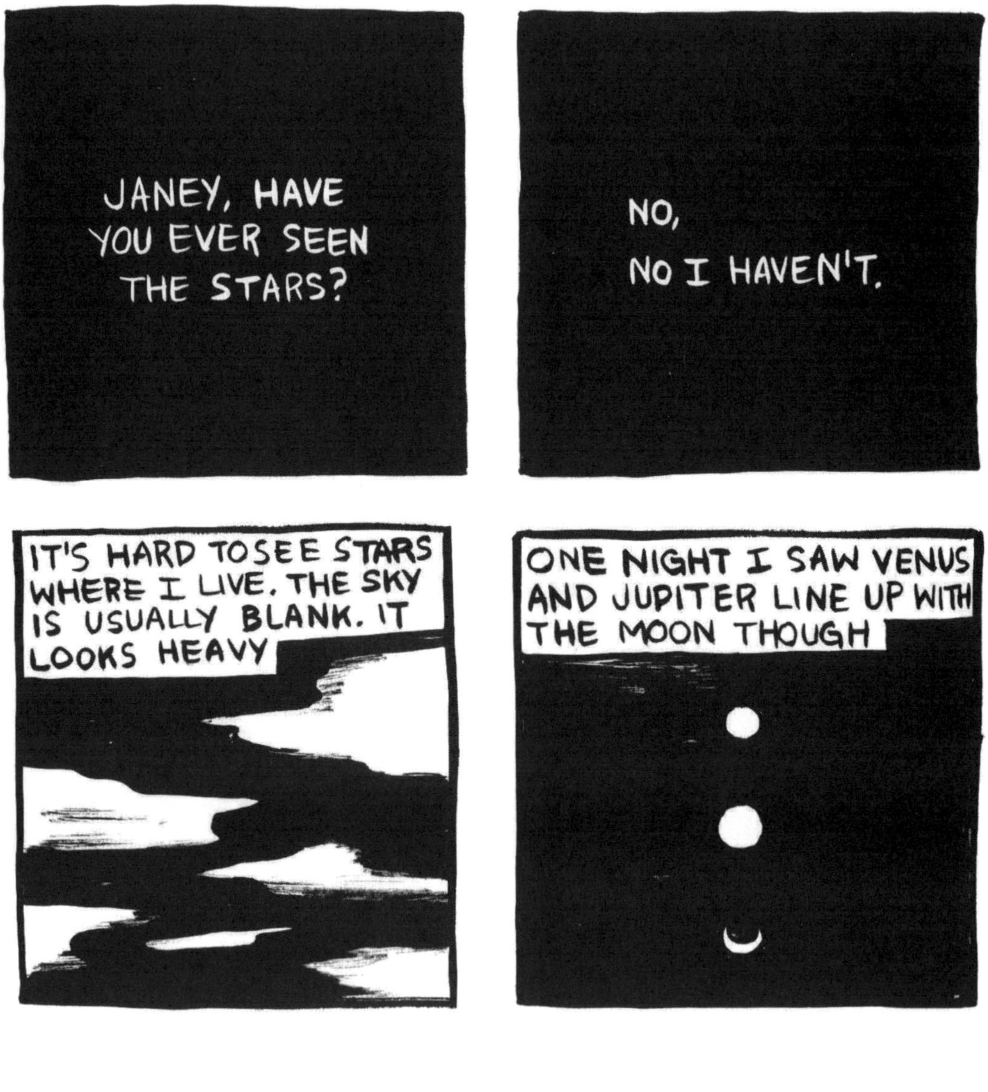
JANEY, HAVE YOU EVER SEEN THE STARS?
NO,
NO I HAVEN'T.
IT'S HARD TOSEE STARS WHERE I LIVE. THE SKY IS USUALLY BLANK. IT LOOKS HEAVY
ONE NIGHT I SAW VENUS AND JUPITER LINE UP WITH THE MOON THOUGH

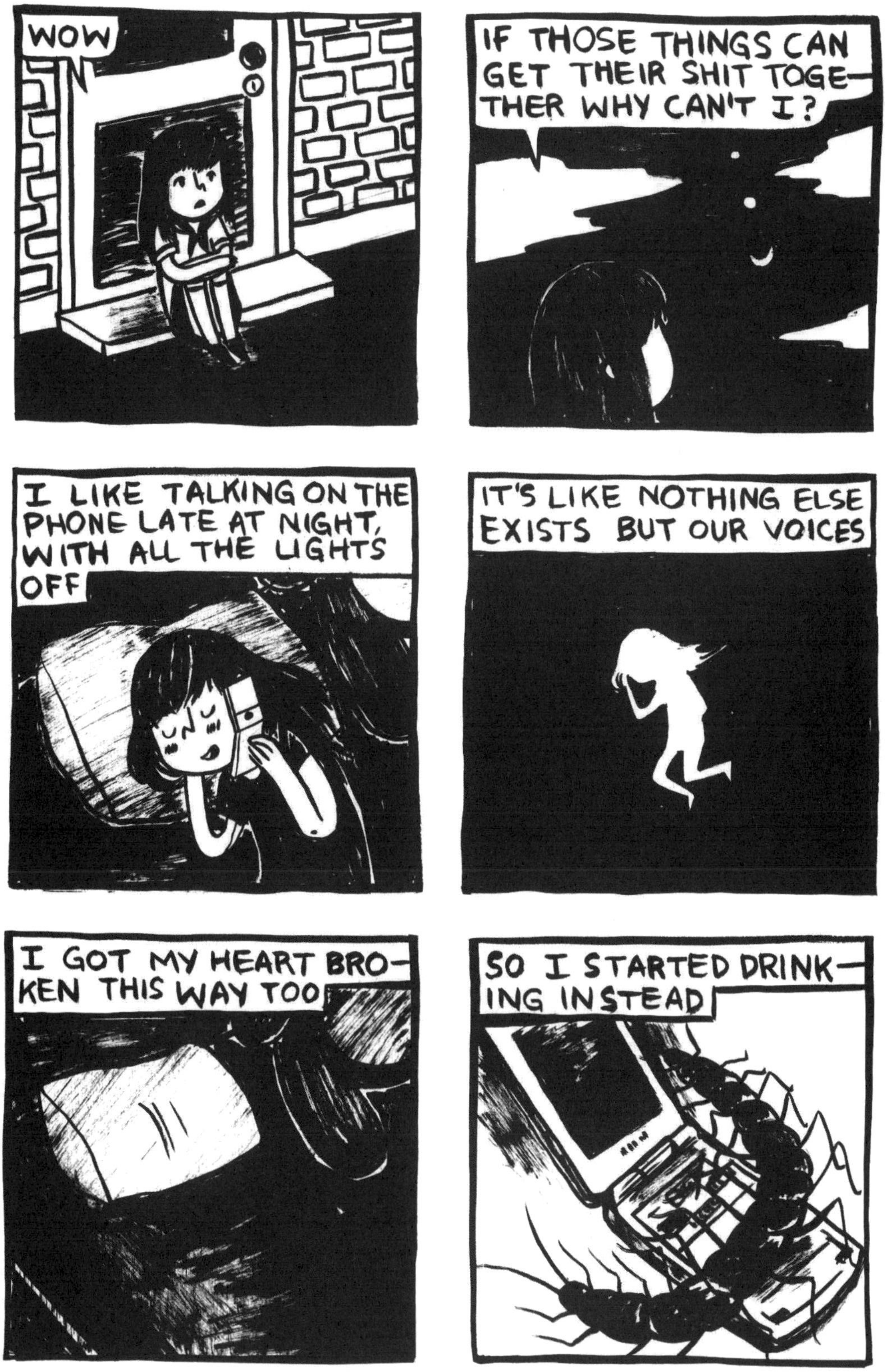
WOW
IF THOSE THINGS CAN GET THEIR SHIT TOGETHER WHY CAN'T I?
I LIKE TALKING ON THE PHONE LATE AT NIGHT, WITH ALL THE LIGHTS OFF
IT'S LIKE NOTHING ELSE EXISTS BUT OUR VOICES
I GOT MY HEART BROKEN THIS WAY TOO
SO I STARTED DRINKING INSTEAD

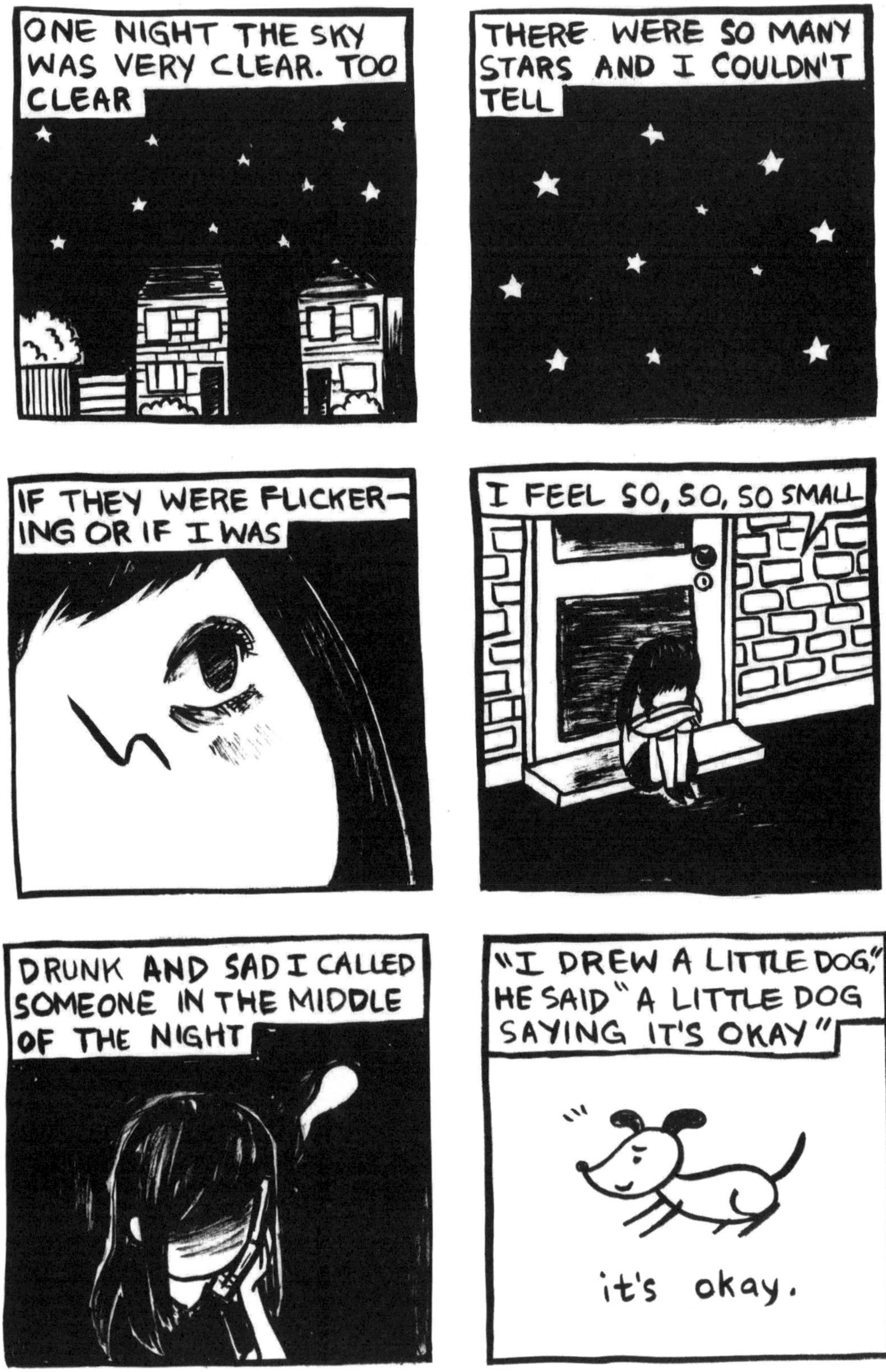
ONE NIGHT THE SKY WAS VERY CLEAR. TOO CLEAR
THERE WERE SO MANY STARS AND I COULDN'T TELL
IF THEY WERE FLICKER-ING OR IF I WAS
I FEEL SO, SO, SO SMALL
DRUNK AND SAD I CALLED SOMEONE IN THE MIDDLE OF THE NIGHT
"I DREW A LITTLE DOG," HE SAID "A LITTLE DOG SAYING IT'S OKAY"
it's okay.

IT'S OKAY EVERYTHING'S GONNA BE OKAY
don't cry kitty cat
DO YOU LOVE ME?
"I DO"
WHERE ARE YOU? WHERE ARE YOU?
i'm scared
I CAN'T SEE CANIS MINOR FROM HERE

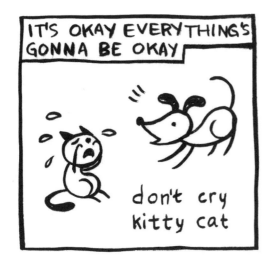

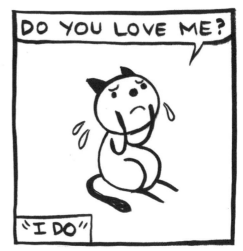

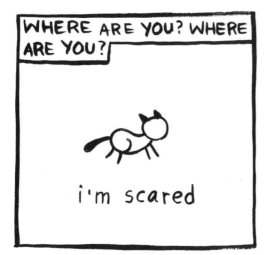

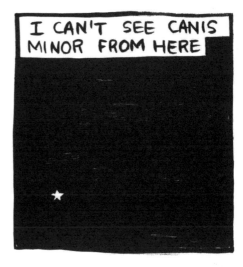

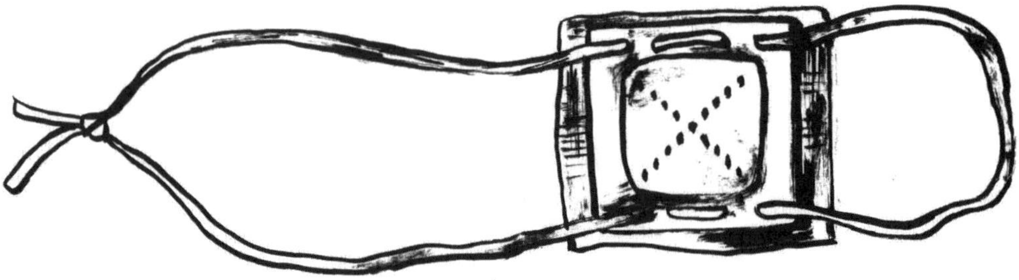

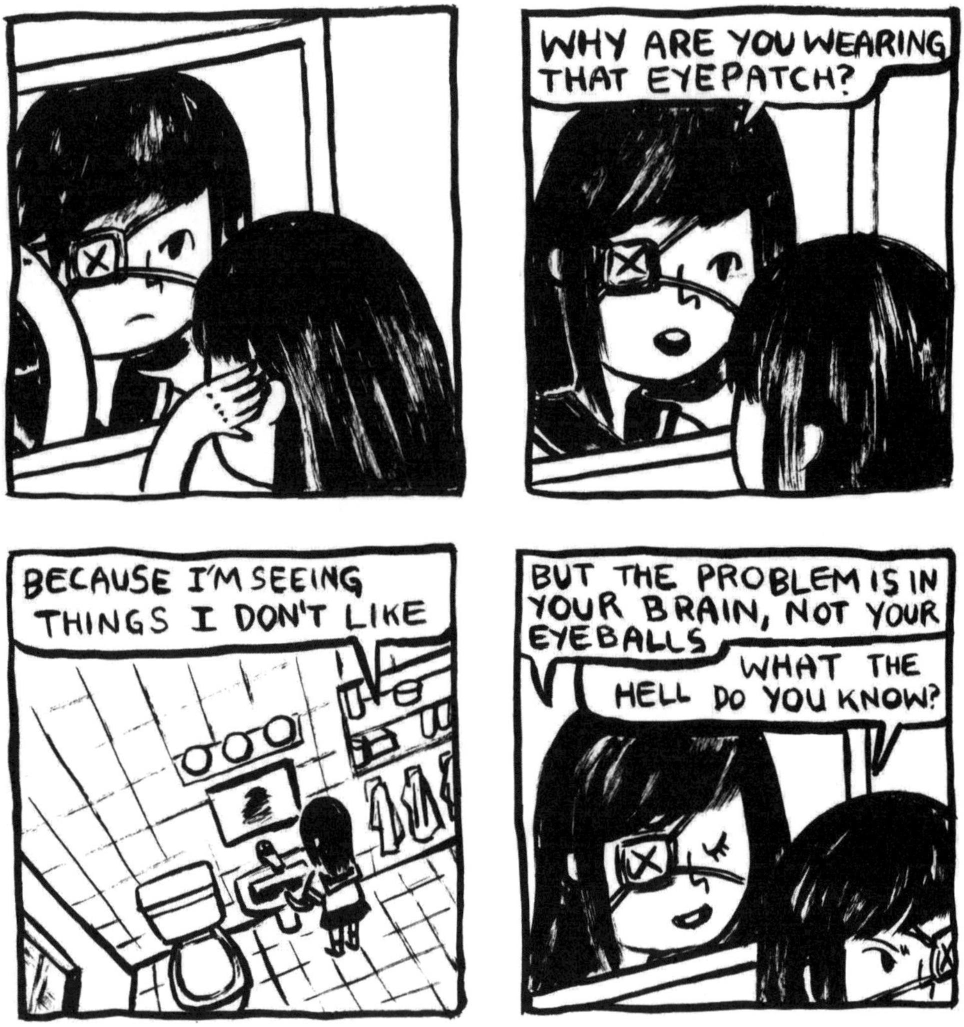
WHY ARE YOU WEARING THAT EYEPATCH?
BECAUSE I'M SEEING THINGS I DON'T LIKE
BUT THE PROBLEM IS IN YOUR BRAIN, NOT YOUR EYEBALLS
WHAT THE HELL DO YOU KNOW?

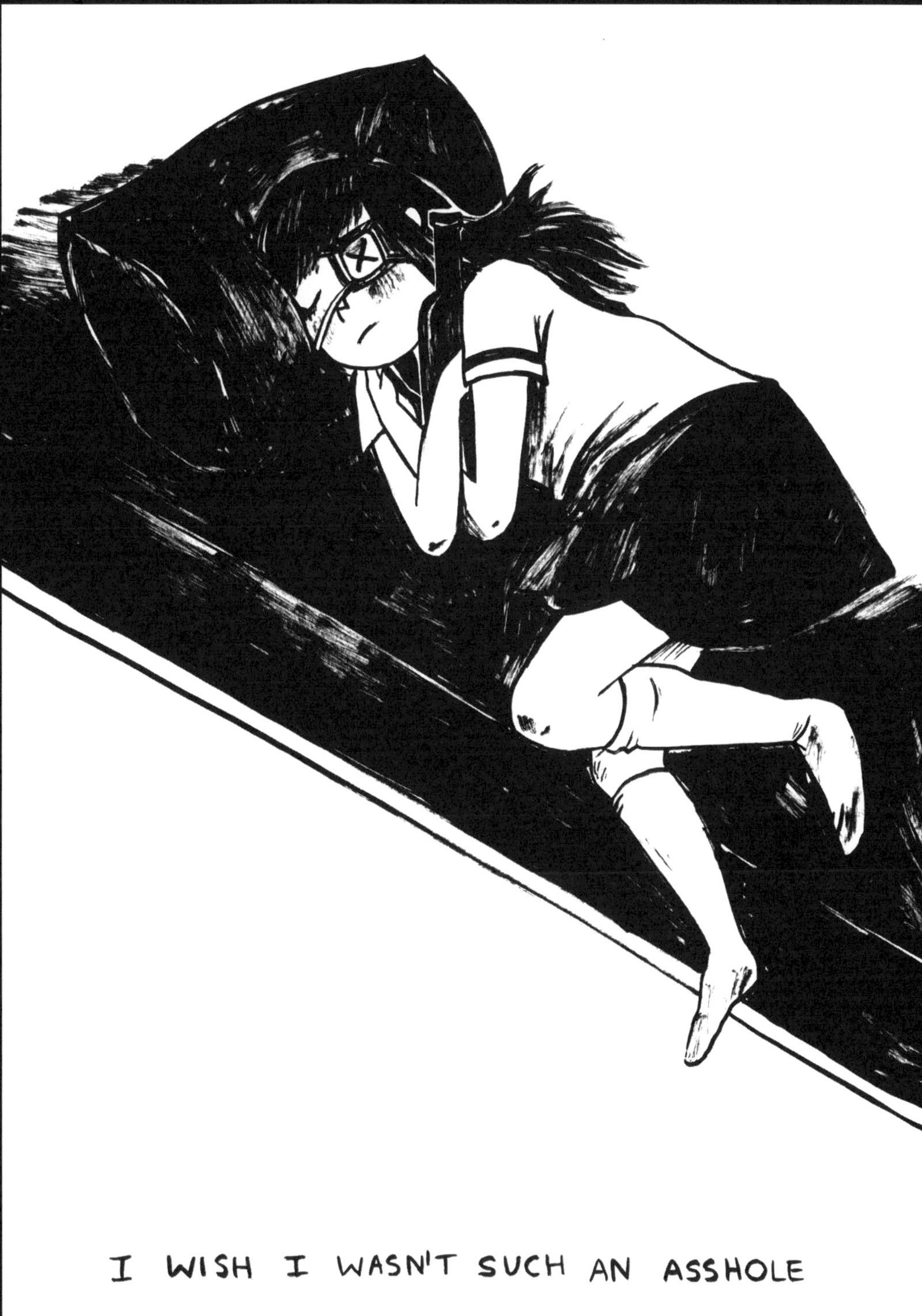
I WISH I WASN'T SUCH AN ASSHOLE

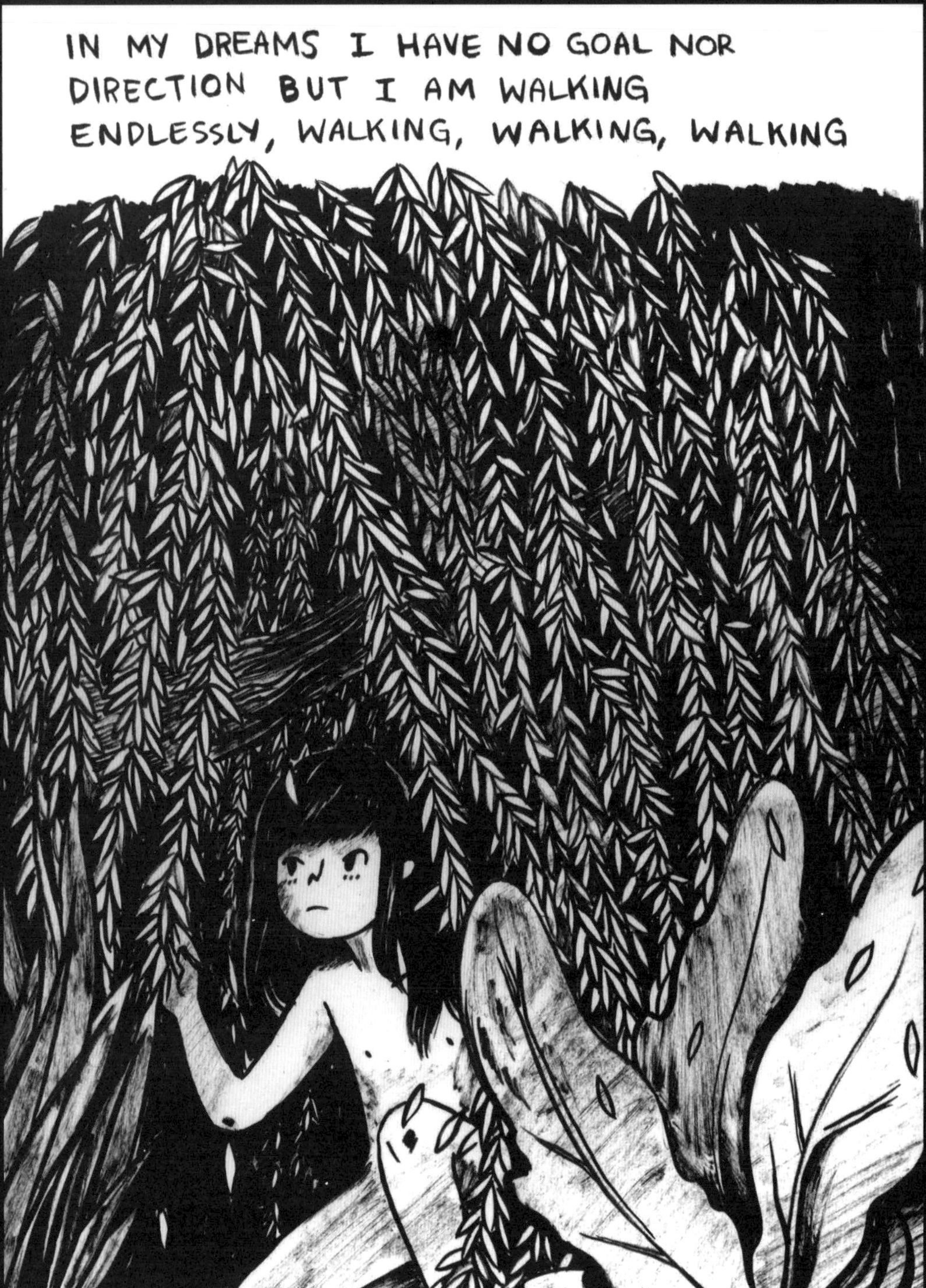
IN MY DREAMS I HAVE NO GOAL NOR DIRECTION BUT I AM WALKING ENDLESSLY, WALKING, WALKING, WALKING

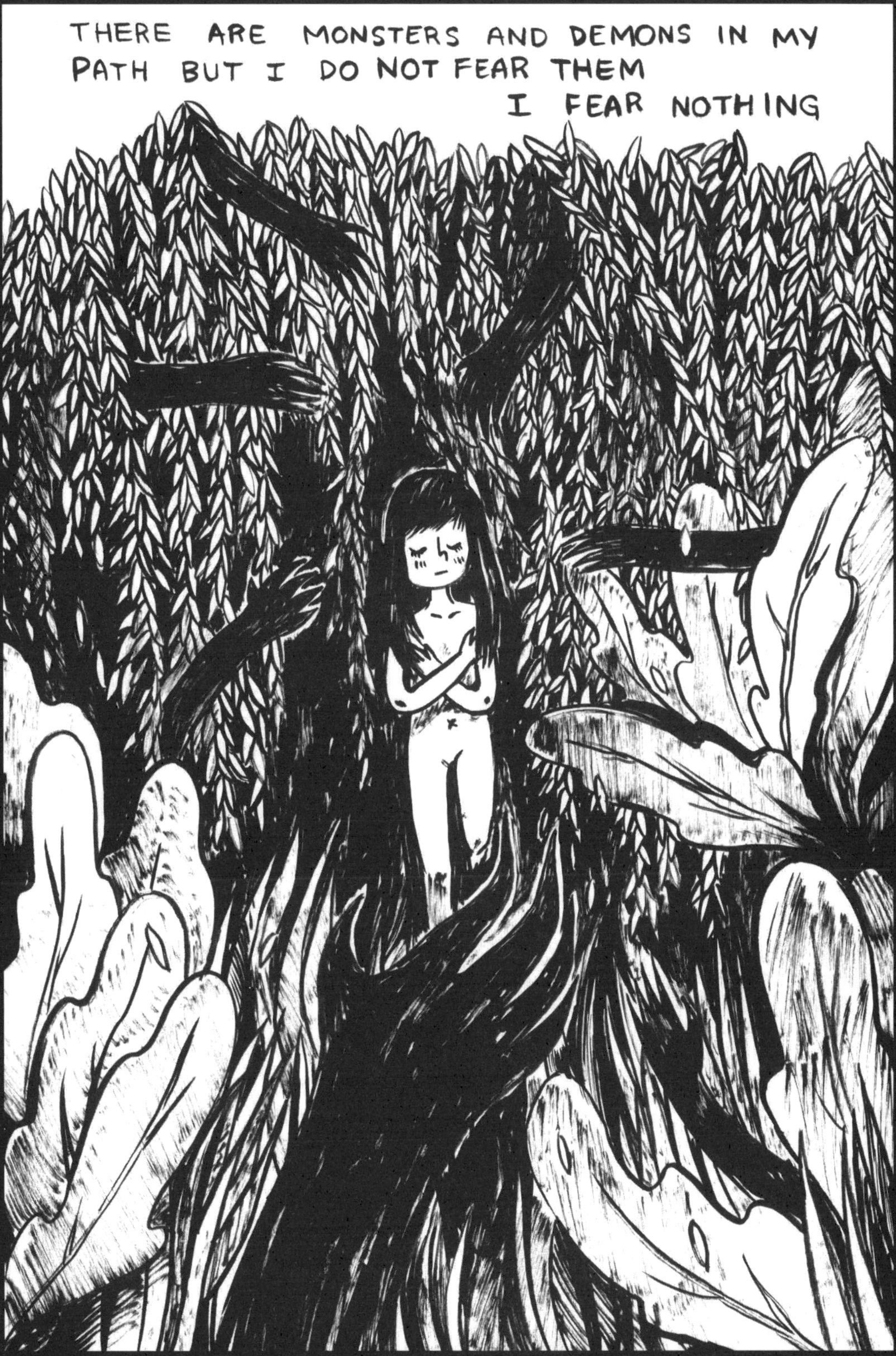
THERE ARE MONSTERS AND DEMONS IN MY PATH BUT I DO NOT FEAR THEM
I FEAR NOTHING

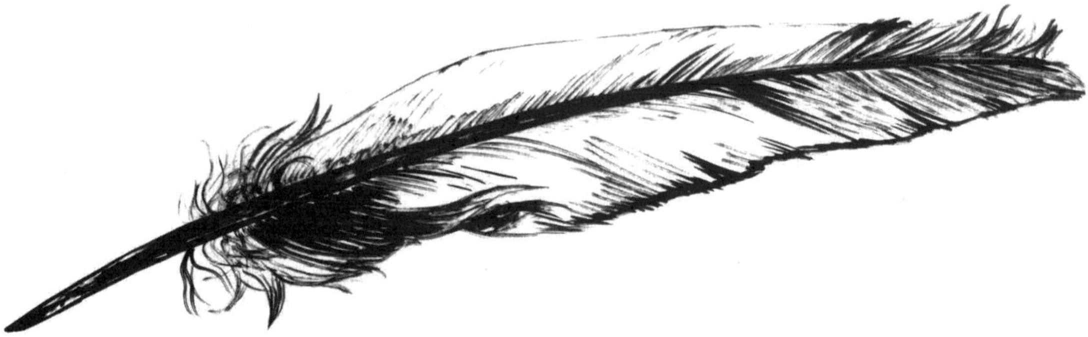

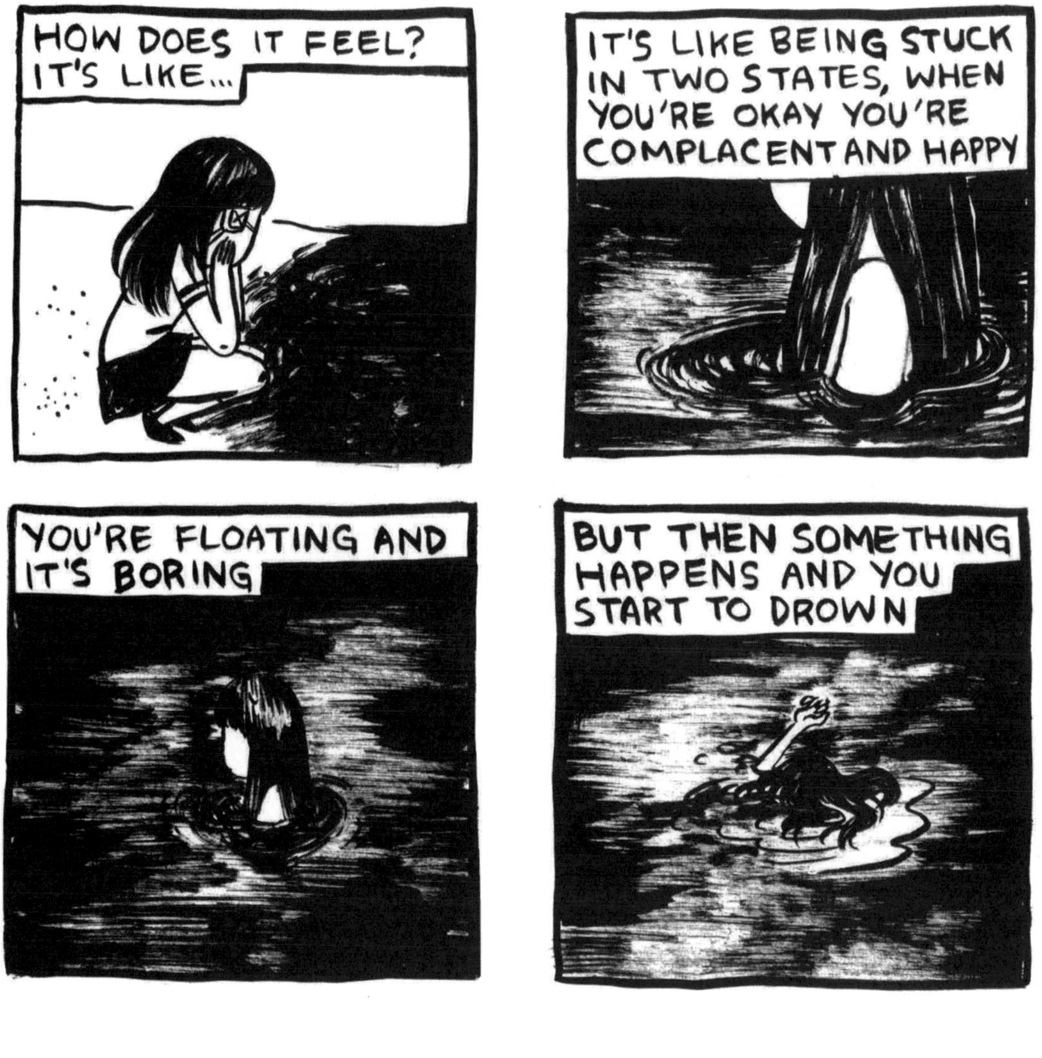
HOW DOES IT FEEL? IT'S LIKE...
IT'S LIKE BEING STUCK IN TWO STATES, WHEN YOU'RE OKAY YOU'RE COMPLACENT AND HAPPY
YOU'RE FLOATING AND IT'S BORING
BUT THEN SOMETHING HAPPENS AND YOU START TO DROWN

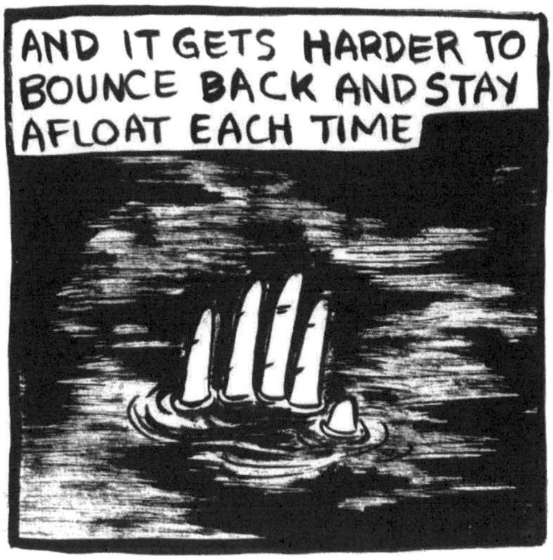
AND IT GETS HARDER TO BOUNCE BACK AND STAY AFLOAT EACH TIME

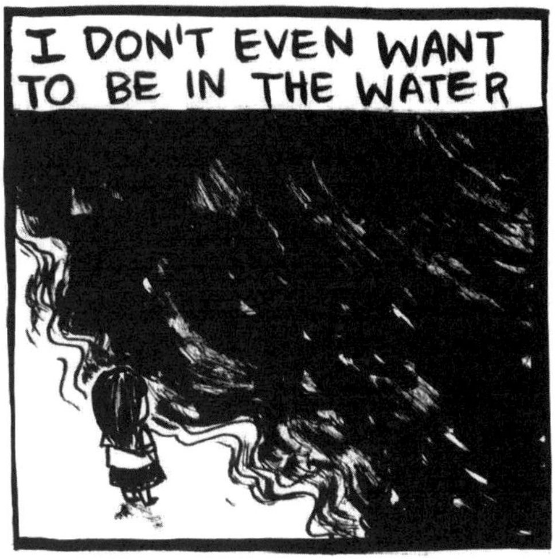
I DON'T EVEN WANT TO BE IN THE WATER

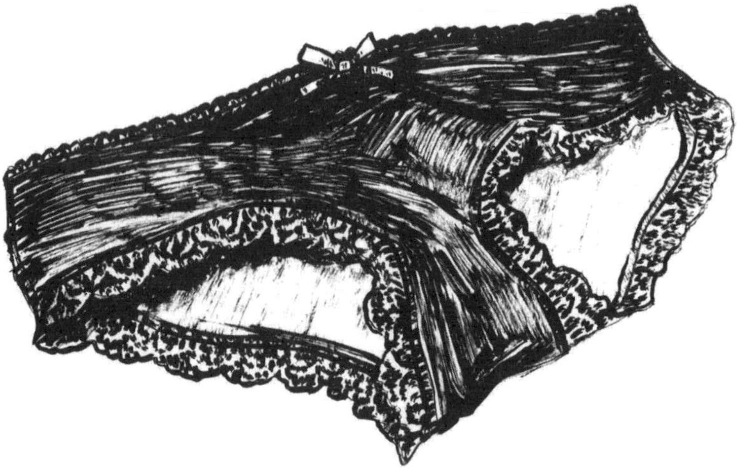

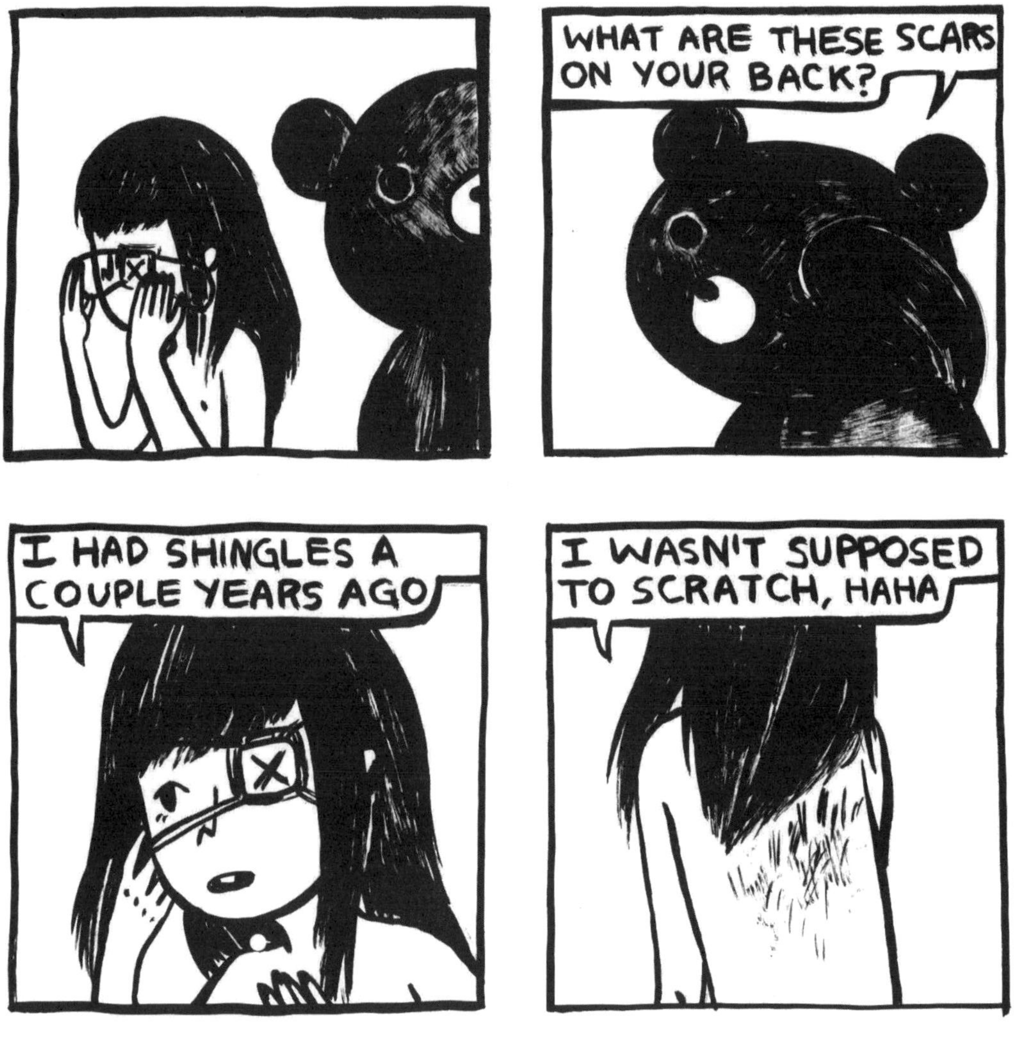
WHAT ARE THESE SCARS ON YOUR BACK?
I HAD SHINGLES A COUPLE YEARS AGO
I WASN'T SUPPOSED TO SCRATCH, HAHA

THESE LOOK NEW
I STILL DO IT, I TAKE REALLY HOT BATHS AND SCRATCH
MAYBE I'M TRYING TO REMOVE PART OF MYSELF
I'M TRYING TO COME OUT OF MY SKIN

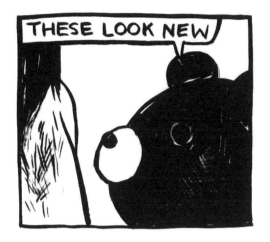

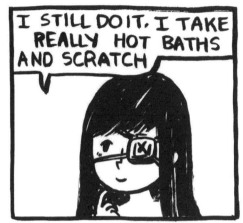

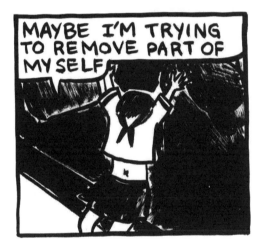

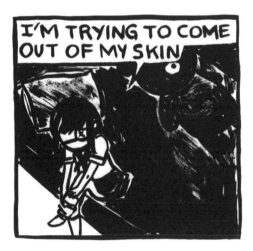

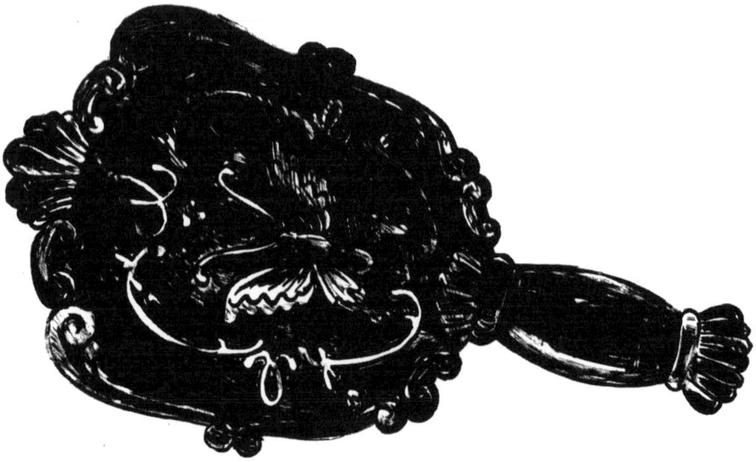

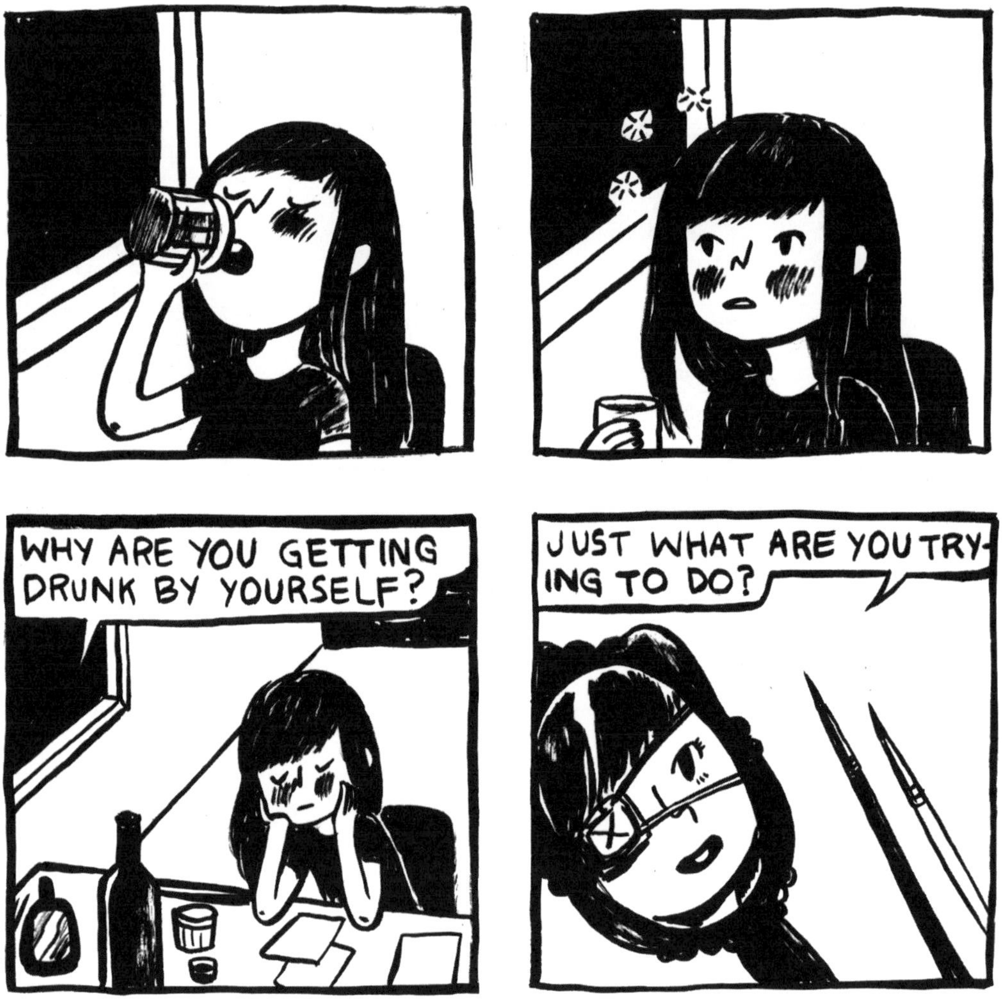
WHY ARE YOU GETTING DRUNK BY YOURSELF?
JUST WHAT ARE YOU TRY-ING TO DO?

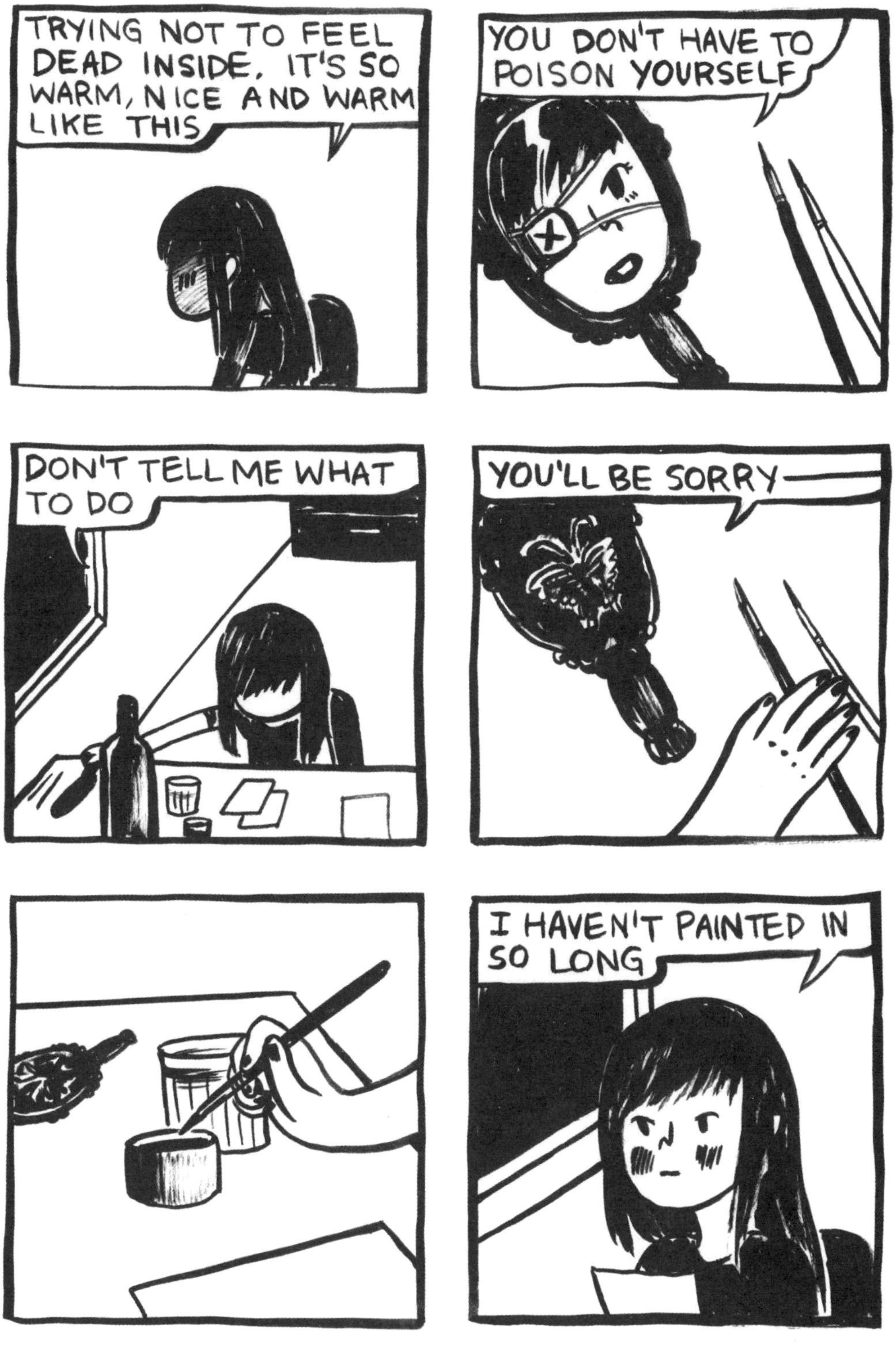
TRYING NOT TO FEEL DEAD INSIDE. IT'S SO WARM, NICE AND WARM LIKE THIS
YOU DON'T HAVE TO POISON YOURSELF
DON'T TELL ME WHAT TO DO
YOU'LL BE SORRY
I HAVEN'T PAINTED IN SO LONG

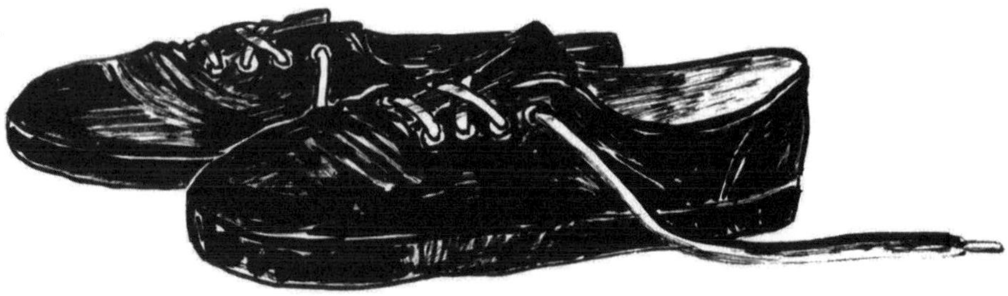

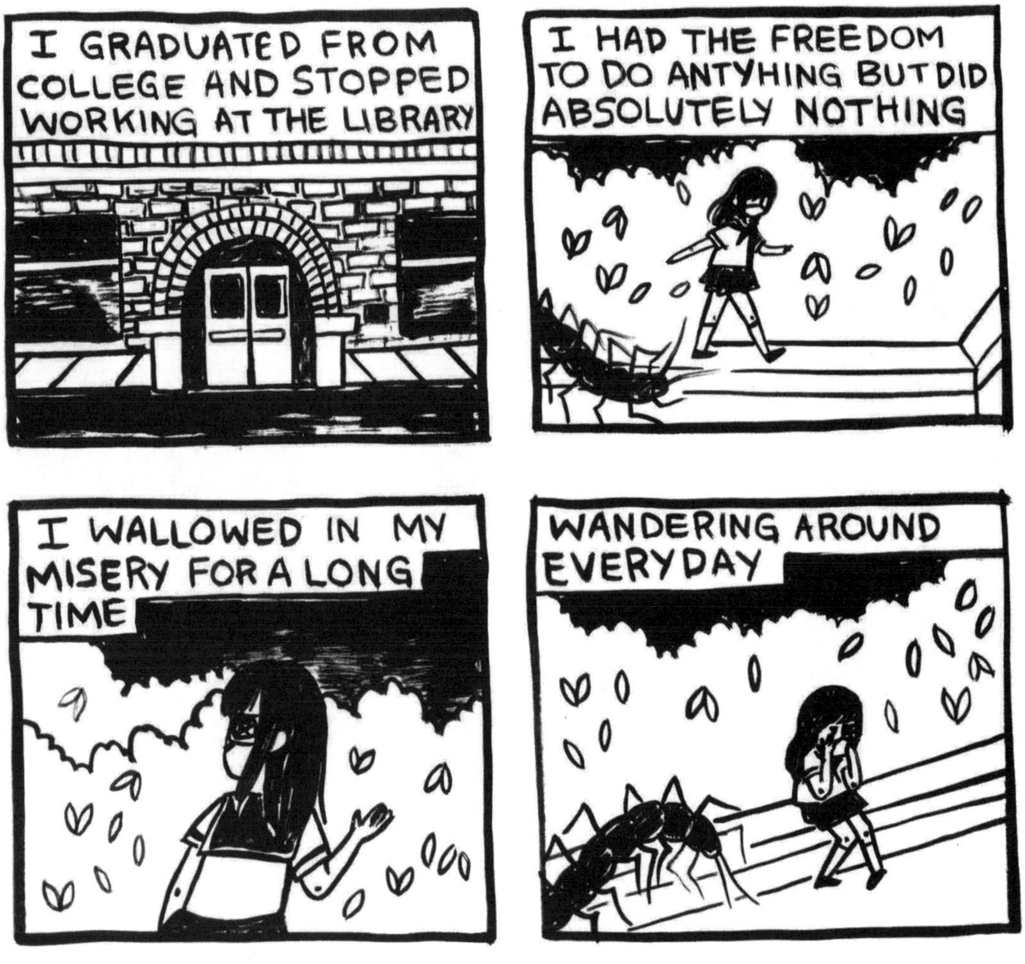
I GRADUATED FROM COLLEGE AND STOPPED WORKING AT THE LIBRARY
I HAD THE FREEDOM TO DO ANTYHING BUT DID ABSOLUTELY NOTHING
I WALLOWED IN MY MISERY FOR A LONG TIME
WANDERING AROUND EVERYDAY

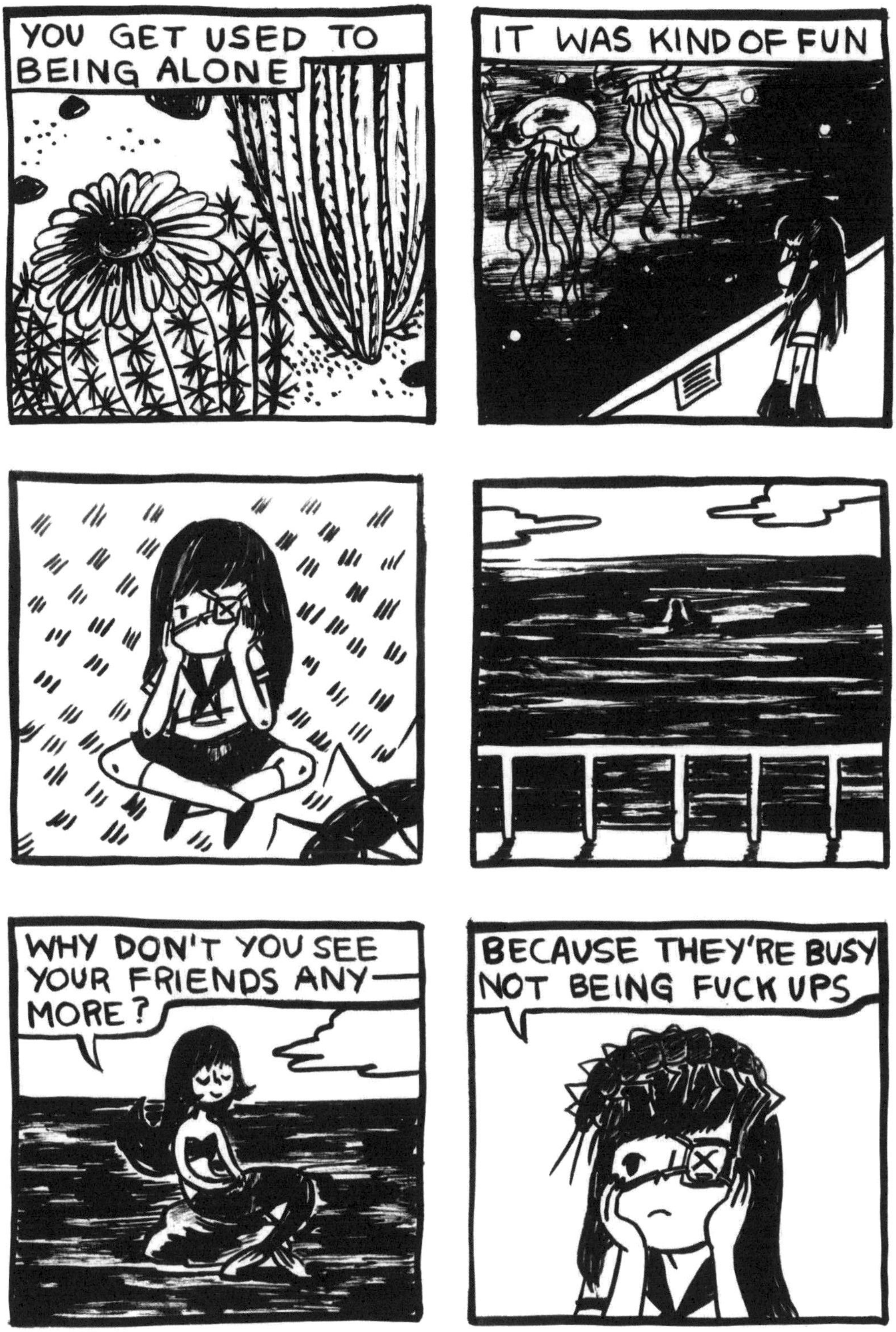
YOU GET USED TO BEING ALONE
IT WAS KIND OF FUN
WHY DON'T YOU SEE YOUR FRIENDS ANY-MORE?
BECAUSE THEY'RE BUSY NOT BEING FUCK UPS

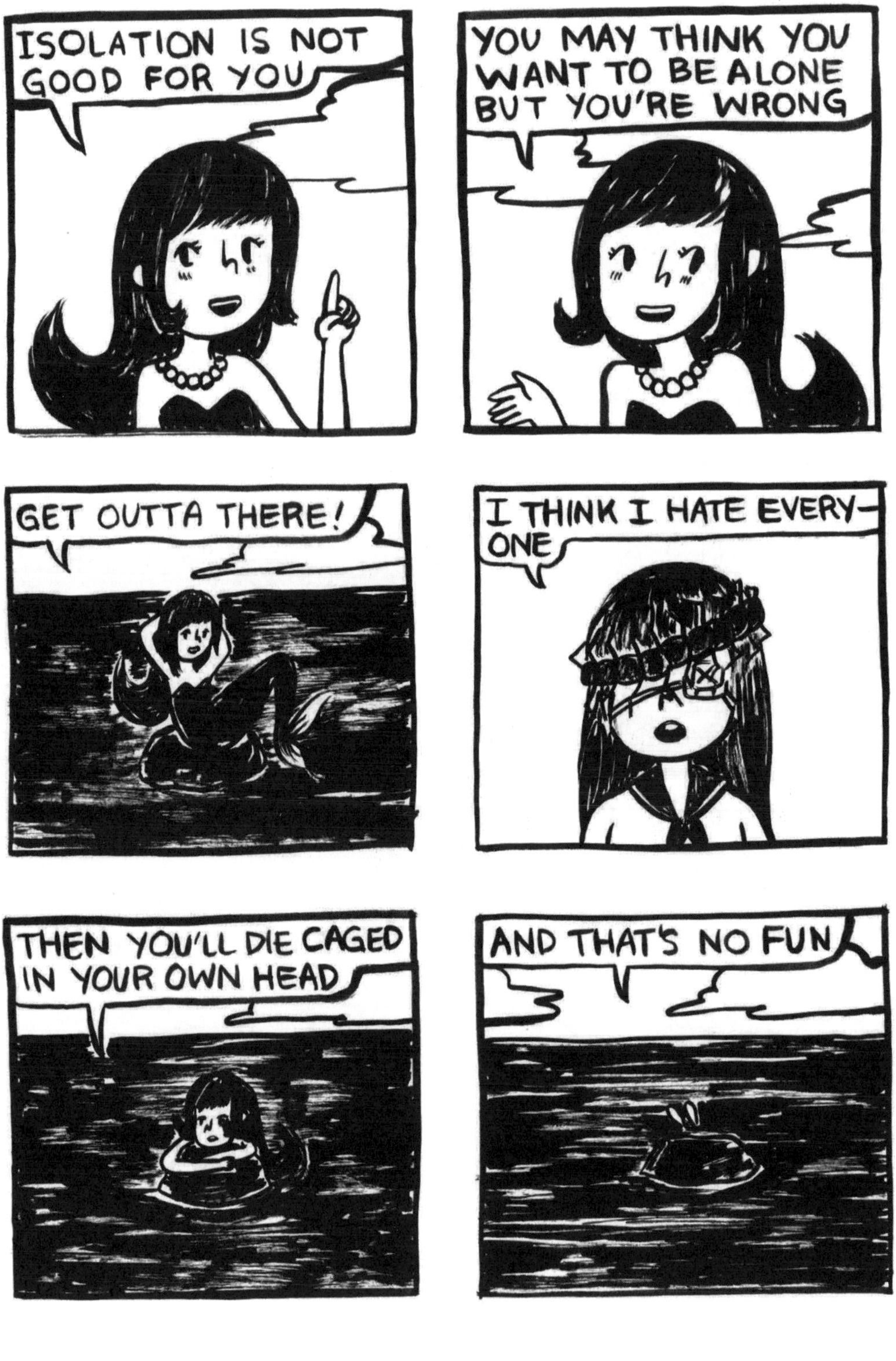
ISOLATION IS NOT GOOD FOR YOU
YOU MAY THINK YOU WANT TO BE ALONE BUT YOU'RE WRONG
GET OUTTA THERE!
I THINK I HATE EVERY-ONE
THEN YOU'LL DIE CAGED IN YOUR OWN HEAD
AND THAT'S NO FUN

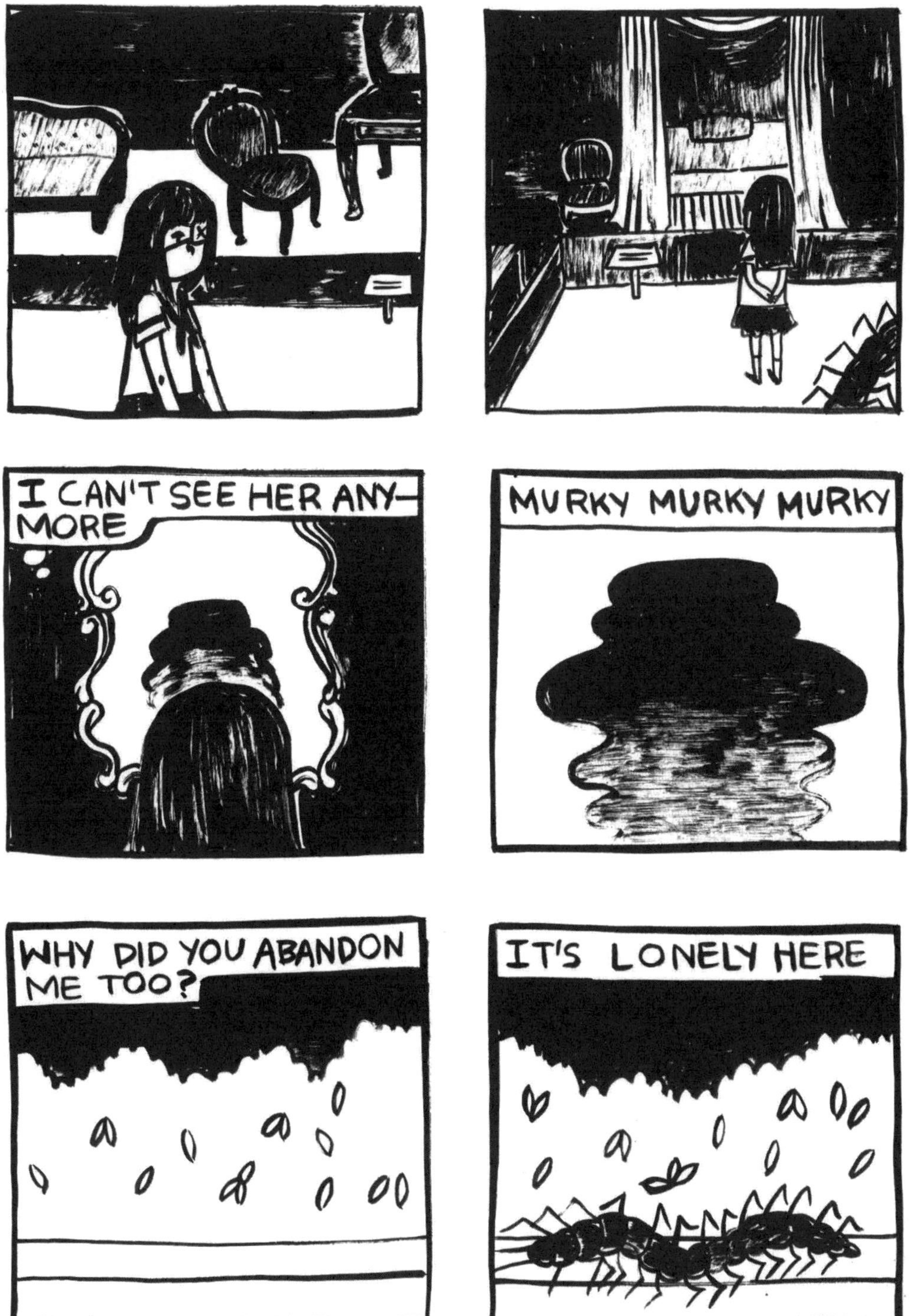

I CAN'T SEE HER ANY-
MORE
MURKY MURKY MURKY
WHY DID YOU ABANDON
ME TOO?
IT'S LONELY HERE

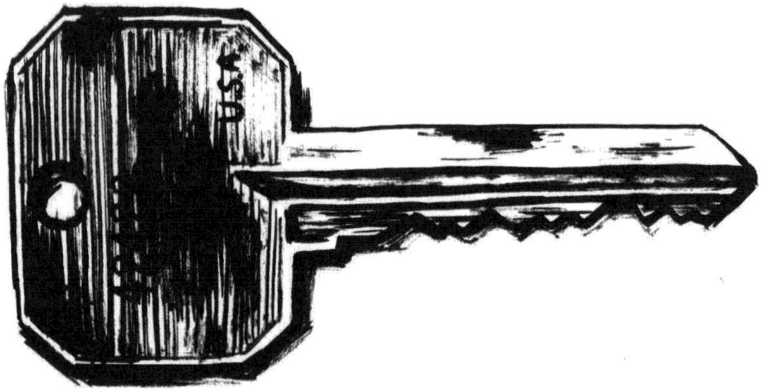
USA

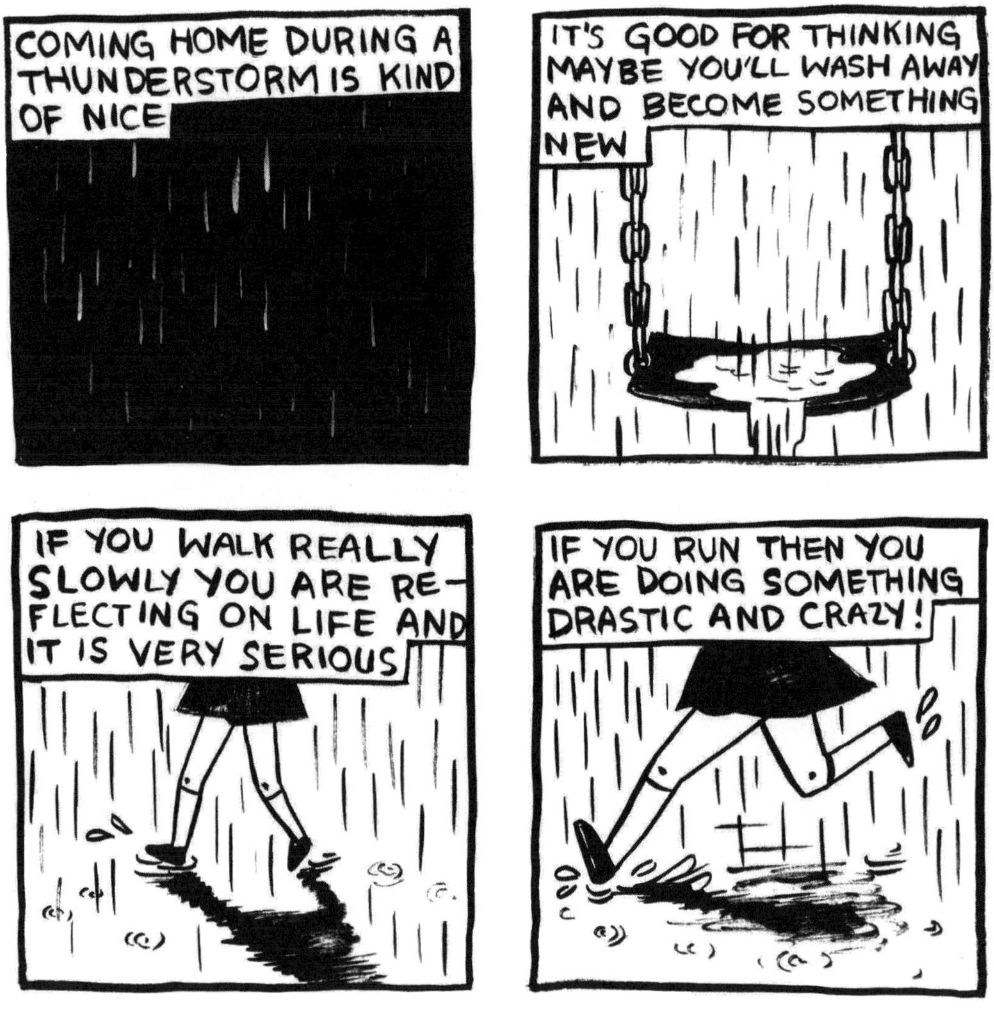
COMING HOME DURING A THUNDERSTORM IS KIND OF NICE
IT'S GOOD FOR THINKING MAYBE YOU'LL WASH AWAY AND BECOME SOMETHING NEW
IF YOU WALK REALLY SLOWLY YOU ARE RE-FLECTING ON LIFE AND IT IS VERY SERIOUS
IF YOU RUN THEN YOU ARE DOING SOMETHING DRASTIC AND CRAZY!

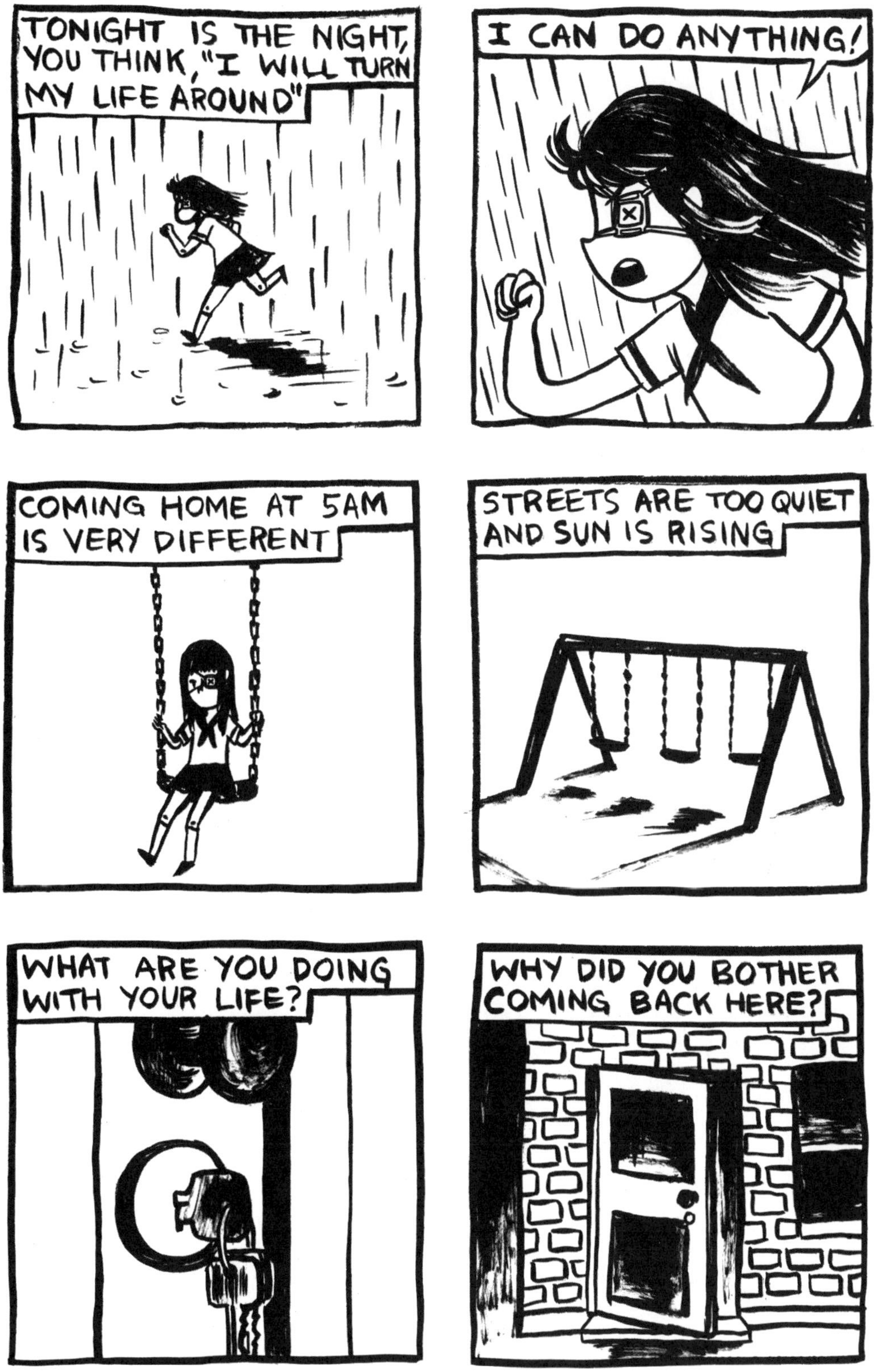
TONIGHT IS THE NIGHT, YOU THINK, "I WILL TURN MY LIFE AROUND"
I CAN DO ANYTHING!
COMING HOME AT 5AM IS VERY DIFFERENT
STREETS ARE TOO QUIET AND SUN IS RISING
WHAT ARE YOU DOING WITH YOUR LIFE?
WHY DID YOU BOTHER COMING BACK HERE?

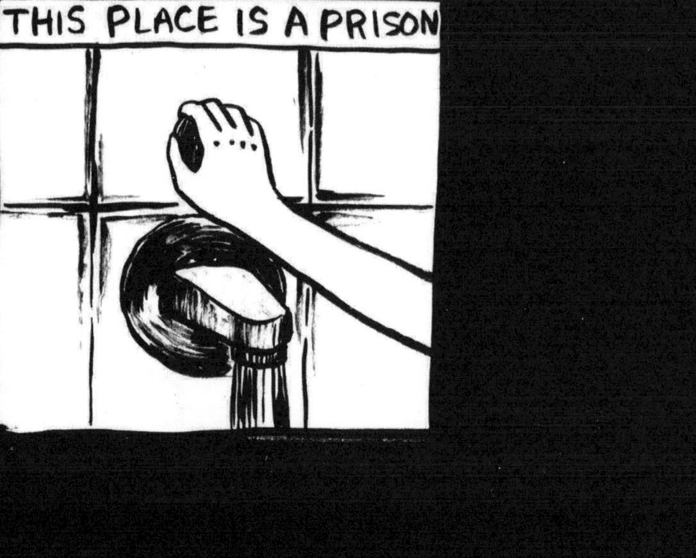
THIS PLACE IS A PRISON

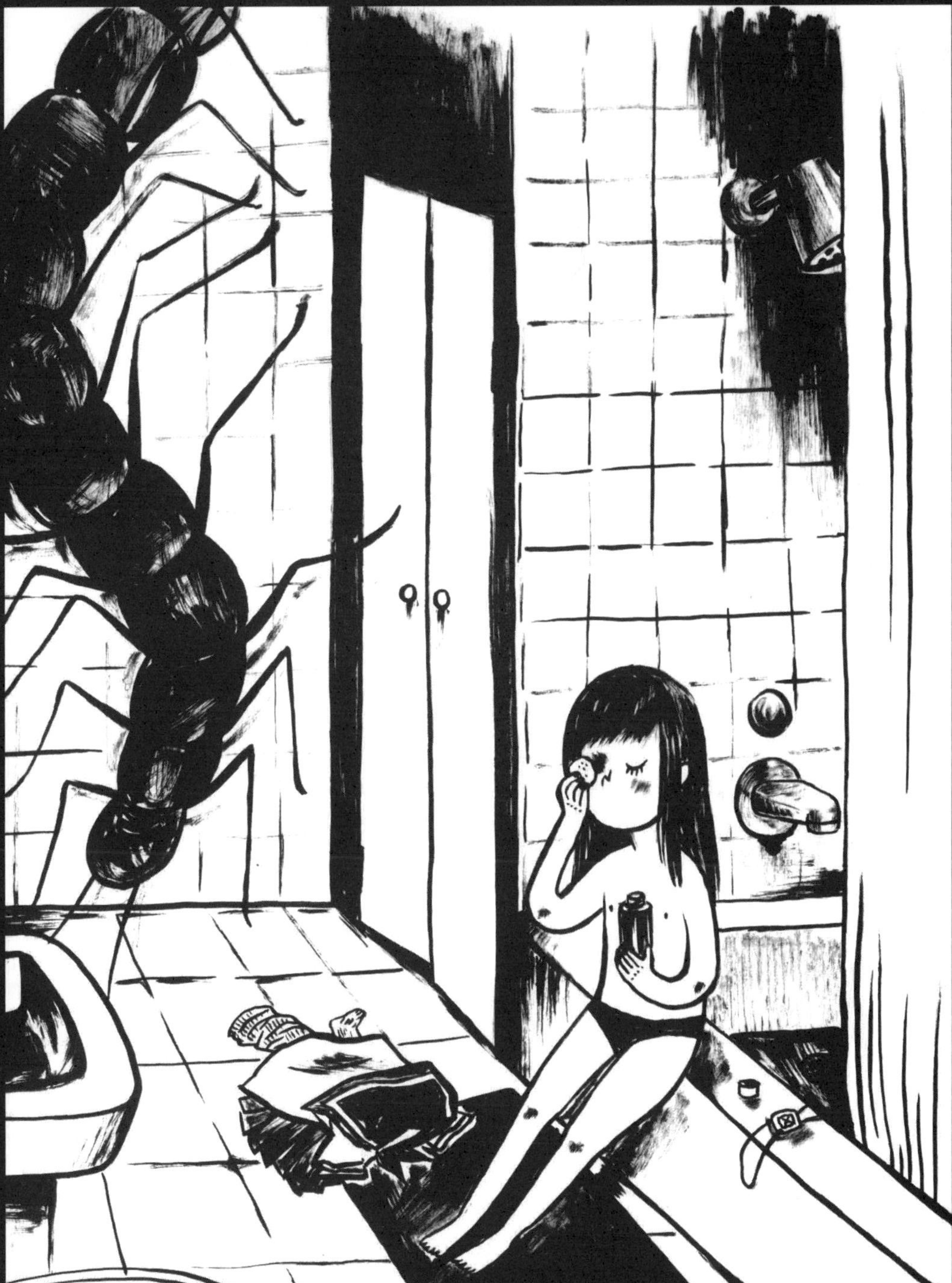

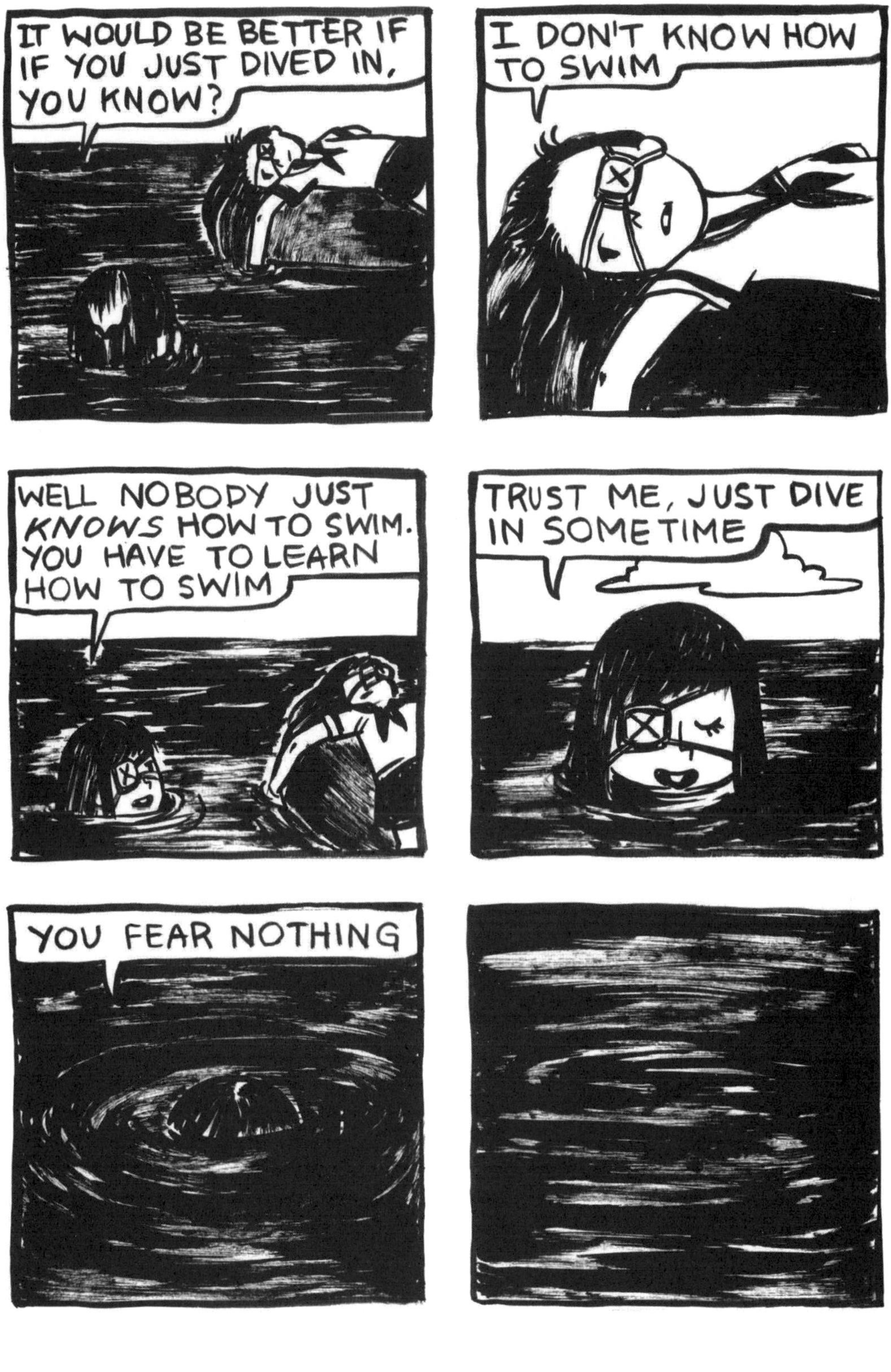
IT WOULD BE BETTER IF IF YOU JUST DIVED IN, YOU KNOW?
I DON'T KNOW HOW TO SWIM
WELL NOBODY JUST *KNOWS* HOW TO SWIM. YOU HAVE TO LEARN HOW TO SWIM
TRUST ME, JUST DIVE IN SOMETIME
YOU FEAR NOTHING

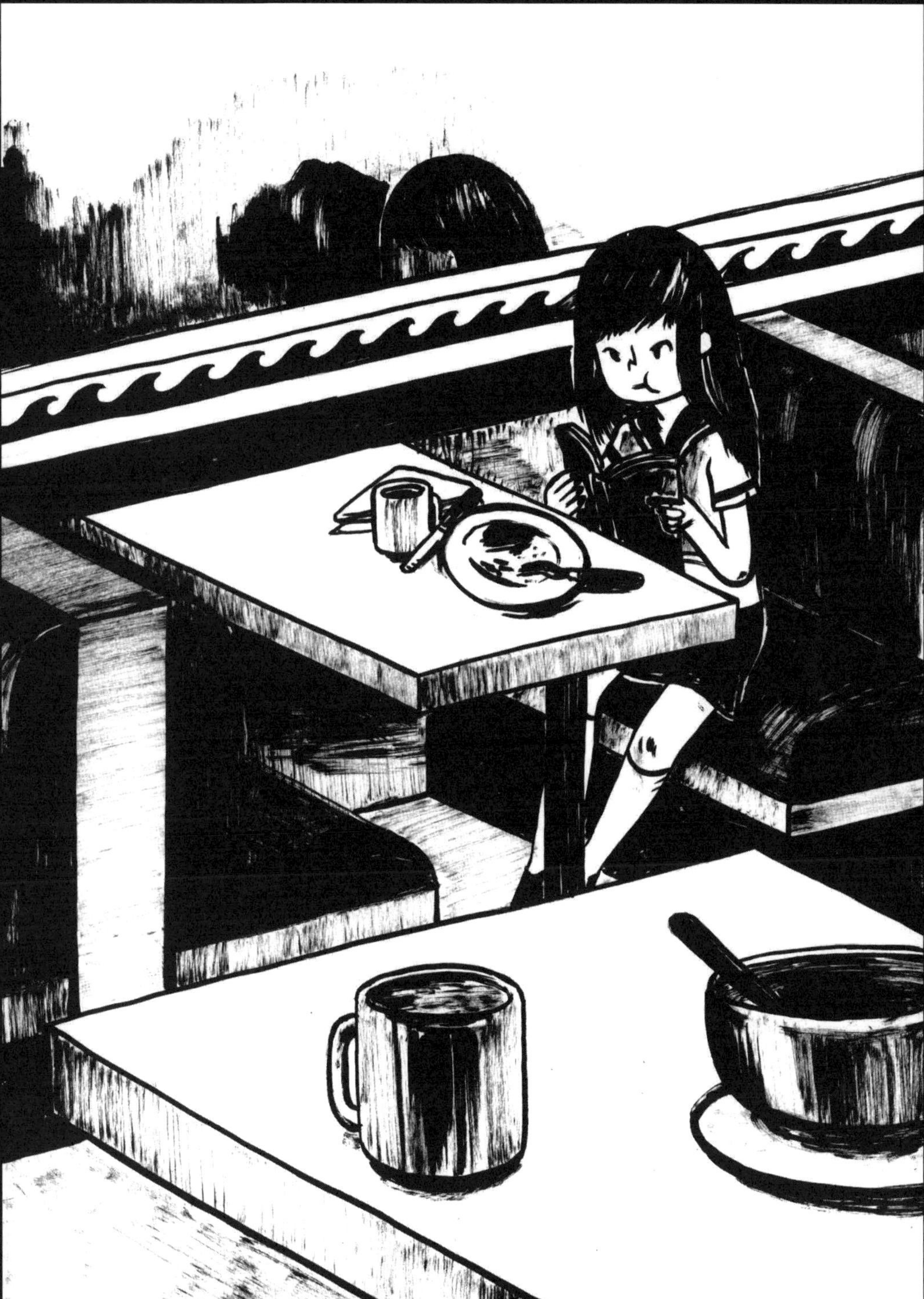

EVERYTHING IS
GONNA BE

OKAY